THE GERMAN MIND

Other books by George F. Wieland

Changing Hospitals

Organization Theory and Design

Improving Health Care Management

Bessarabian Knight

Celtic Germans: The Rise and Fall of Ann Arbor's Swabians

Stubborn & Liking It: Einstein & Other Germans

Escape from Hell: German Voices

THE GERMAN MIND

MADE FOR INDUSTRY?

George F. Wieland, Ph.D.

ANN ARBOR, MICHIGAN

Copyright © 2018 George F. Wieland

All rights reserved. Except as permitted under the U. S. Copyright Act of 1976, no part of this publication may be reproduced, distributed, transmitted in any form or by any means, or stored in a database or retrieval system, without the prior written permission from the author, George F. Wieland at gwieland@umich.edu.

ISBN-13:
978-1718766228

ISBN-10:
171876622X

On the cover: The German flag colors

PREFACE

Many people have helped me over the years that it took to do the research for my series of books about Germans and Germany.. I'm very grateful to all the people who shared their minds with me. Many graciously took time to answer my sometimes ignorant questions.

The late Prof. Heinz Biesdorf of Cornell University and his wife, Ellen, entertained me over the years with stories about Germans. I was also encouraged by visits to Prof. Ulrich Planck at the Universität Hohenheim, as well as Prof. Martin Scharfe, Prof. Hermann Bausinger, and the late Prof. Utz Jeggle—all at the Universität Tübingen—and the late Dr. Paul Sauer, historian and head of the state archives in Stuttgart.

Michael Betzold copyedited my manuscript, trying to fix my Germanic syntax. My readers over the years have been helpful not only in correcting drafts but also in providing encouragement: Dr. Barbara K. Petersen, Patience S. Wieland, Charlie Zakrajshek, Dr. Elaine Hockman, Dr. James Wahl, and Sharon Kane Wieland. They are not responsible for the inevitable errors and infelicities that remain.

The University of Michigan and Ann Arbor District libraries obtained many books for me with interlibrary loans.

Finally, Nancy Shattuck of Wayne State University provided needed encouragement when I was overwhelmed with computer and publication problems.

CONTENTS

INTRODUCTION 11

1: STEREOTYPES 17

2: OBJECTIVE DATA ABOUT GERMANS 25

3: EXTRAVERSION-INTROVERSION 31

4: AGREEABLENESS-DISAGREEABLENESS 37

5: CONSCIENTIOUSNESS 43

6: OPENNESS 51

7: NEUROTICISM 55

8: CULTURES 73

9: WARS 91

10: TERROR MANAGEMENT AND NORMS 97

11: PERSONALITY VS. CULTURE 101

CONCLUSIONS 103

REFERENCES 105

INDEX **121**

THE AUTHOR... **129**

INTRODUCTION

Germany is the world's fourth-strongest economic power in the world, behind only the United States, Japan, and China, all with many more people than Germany. For 150 years Germany has surpassed most countries in economic prowess despite devastating wars, political strife, and shrinking territory. Why? Perhaps it's because of the psychology and culture of the German people. In this book I will address the following questions:

Is German economic success due to many German people being workaholics who don't waste time socializing and having fun?

How important is the priority given to obedience in German culture?

Can the German emphasis on order and efficiency explain how Germany outperforms other countries economically?

Why do Germans seem disagreeable in temperament?

Why are punishments rather than rewards often used to control behaviors in Germany?

Germans have long had a reputation as thinkers and philosophers. They seem to love information. Do these traits contribute to Germany's economic achievements?

Does angst, a severe general anxiety that is a distinctive feature of the German psyche, help or hinder achievement?

Could the modern study of epigenetics explain how the repeated traumas of war paradoxically seem to have made Germany even stronger in some ways?

Does the American theory of "terror management" help explain Germany's economic success?

How might East Germany's forty-five years under Communism contribute an understanding of German economic power?

I will also look at some of the peculiarities of German culture: Why do Germans prefer to do one thing at a time rather than multitask? Is the German dislike of uncertainty a factor in economic achievement?

Why are many Germans reluctant to smile?

Why do they suffer from negativism and hypochondria?

THE GERMAN MIND

Why do Germans love to criticize but also love to take criticisms from others?

Why are Germans more pessimistic about the future than people in other countries despite their nation's strong economy?

Why are they politically conservative?

Why do they suffer from what some call "paralysis by analysis?"

And why did the German equivalent of *Time* magazine once devote forty pages to a history of the bathroom?

A History of Achievement

About 1800, what later became Germany had 300 separate principalities and 1500 semi-autonomous states. This hindered economic cooperation. When the nation was formally created in 1871, Germany took off and quickly approached and then surpassed the two world powers at the time, France and Great Britain. Total output of coal in the Ruhr region grew from 2 million tons in 1850 to 22 million tons in 1880, 60 million tons in 1900, and 114 million tons in 1913.

Over the last three or four generations, Germany has been more productive than other large European nations with comparable natural resources despite twice suffering abject defeat in war. More recently, West Germany annexed Communist East Germany with its mostly backward industries, and German economic power only suffered a brief hiccup.

Germany's defeat in the First World War meant the loss of all its colonies plus the territories of Alsace-Lorraine and West Prussia. Germany also had to pay enormous reparations. In addition, France in 1923 invaded and occupied Germany's primary industrial area, the Ruhr, crippling the country. Subsequently, hyperinflation caused the mark's value to fall from four to a dollar to more than four billion to a dollar. Yet, under Nazi rule starting in 1933, Germany spectacularly recovered economically.

After the Second World War, Germany lost a third of its territory to Poland and the Soviet Union. In West Germany, Allied bombing had devastated industries and housing. Few people were available to work in the mines and other industries. The British allowed rations of only a thousand calories per person in the

INTRODUCTION

industrialized north, resulting in near starvation. Nevertheless, the German people recovered. In what seemed an economic miracle, West Germany in the 1950s became the world's second-greatest economic power after the United States. Truncated West Germany clearly surpassed Britain and France, the war's biggest European victors.

The one-third of Germany that became Communist East Germany was a basket case at the end of the Second World War. It lacked essential natural resources. The Soviet Union removed industrial assets worth over a billion dollars as war reparations. The Soviets also demanded payment for its occupation amounting to about one and a half billion dollars a year. In addition, the Soviet Union ordered ships and other goods, paying much less than the cost to build them. Despite having a quarter of its GNP stripped by the Soviet Union, Communist East Germany also managed its own economic miracle, achieving the highest standard of living of all the Communist nations. The East Germans were even able to export some finely crafted items such as cameras. However, the inefficiencies of the Communist system in East Germany meant that West Germany later had to pour in an enormous amount of money, a trillion dollars, when it absorbed East Germany after the fall of the Wall in 1990. Even so, German economic power suffered only a brief pause.

For 2013, Organisation for Economic Cooperation and Development (OECD) data on gross domestic product per capita showed unified Germany at $42,682, ahead of other major European nations such as France ($37,267), the United Kingdom (36,298)), and Italy ($33, 922).

German corporations have not become strong on the backs of their workers. Starting in the late nineteenth century, Germany set up old age pensions and accident, medical, and unemployment insurance. Such expenditures have continued to grow to the point that government assistance in Germany is today the most generous in the world.

German policy has long emphasized the value of education in creating a more productive work force. Today, half the students in upper secondary schools go on to vocational training, with half of all them taking on apprenticeships. Such foresight is an example of German conscientiousness, which I will discuss in detail in Chapter 5.

Could an abundance of natural resources explain Germany's success? Late in the nineteenth century, Germany had large deposits of coal which was used for its steel industry. But France and England had similarly large amounts of coal. Other German industries have since surpassed its the former steel industry based on the coal and iron: machinery, vehicles, chemical goods, electrical equipment, and pharmaceuticals. And Germany's SAP is the third largest computer software firm in the world.

What accounts for German economic prowess despite its defeats in war and the depletion of coal and other natural resources? In addressing this question, most observers have ignored the psychology and culture of the German people. To take one example, Germans are very frugal. They save rather than spend. The German household savings rate is about 10 percent of gross domestic product, compared to about 3 percent in the US according to the OECD. Not surprisingly, the German word for debt, *Schuld*, also means guilt. If you have to borrow money, Germans feel there is something morally wrong with you. The German propensity for thrift enables the country to have trade surpluses equal to about 8.5 percent of its gross domestic product according to the World Bank. Germany can use this money to buy foreign assets. In contrast, the United States has to borrow from abroad. Frugality is another aspect of conscientiousness. By being frugal, Germans have given their country an advantage over other countries.

This book will examine the German character in terms of the so-called "Big Five" personality syndromes. One syndrome, conscientiousness, is a potential explanation for Germany's success. Conscientiousness includes traits of being organized, orderly, systematic, efficient, precise, prompt, meticulous, and frugal. A second major personality syndrome, neuroticism or anxiety, may also be a factor in German achievements. The propensity to avoid

INTRODUCTION

uncertainty is also a possible explanation for German economic success.

1: STEREOTYPES

Stereotypes of the German people have been commonplace for centuries—though not always consistent over time. In the Napoleonic era, Frenchwoman Germaine de Stael's *De l'Allemagne* is relevant. Apparently she once offered herself to Napoleon as a mistress but was rejected. She then wrote positively about the "poetry of the German soul" and wished that the Frenchmen of her time could emulate the deeper, warmer, and more romantic Germans. Frenchmen were too superficial, too cold, too unromantic. Napoleon was not once mentioned in her book. As a result, he called de Stael a whore—and an ugly one, too.[1] (superscript numbers refer to sources listed at the end of this book.)

During the Second World War, American psychologists often asserted that Germans were very aggressive people. These psychologists were not immune to biased selection of data. Even today, it's easy to find jokes online based on negative stereotypes of Germans. For example, "Have you heard about the new German-Chinese restaurant? The food is great, but an hour later, you're hungry for power." A 1978 drama by a Scottish playwright asserts: "One German makes a philosopher, two a public meeting, three a war."

For a long time after the Second World War there were many biased psychological studies of German character.[2] And Hollywood often continued to portray Germans as aggressive Nazi types even though Germany refused to join the U.S. invasion of Iraq nor its overthrow of Muammar Gaddafi in Libya. Of course, there is some validity to stereotypes.[3] But, as we will see, objective scientific studies by anthropologists, psychologists, and other social scientists paint a different picture.

Stereotypes of Germans have also changed over time, as would be expected given political events. In 1933, Americans ranked "extremely nationalistic" sixth highest in a list of descriptive adjectives applicable to Germans. The Second World War boosted that description to third highest in 1951 and fourth highest in 1969. But by 1978, "extremely nationalist" was ranked only seventeenth highest.[4]

In a 1977 study examining aggression in children, four-year-olds were asked to tell stories using toys. Compared to Americans, the German children told less aggressive stories with more friendly characters, using less aggressive words and less physical aggression. Aggressiveness seemed to have lessened in Germany. Or, did American aggressiveness increase?[5]

Obedient Germans

The obedient German is another common stereotype. Is Germany a well-oiled machine where superiors command and Germans do what they are told? Certainly German economic prowess during the 1930s plus the continued productivity during the Second World War despite Allied bombing was created by the Nazi command economy.

Sigmund Freud felt that authoritarianism resulted from a son resolving the Oedipal father-son conflict by identifying with the controlling father. During the Second World War, American Freudian psychologists characterized Germans as having a strong need to obey, worship, and sacrifice. Surveys after the war seemed to confirm Freud's theory. Interviews in 1945 of Germans from nineteen to seventy years of age showed that authoritarianism held fast over the generations. The German father was considered omnipotent, omniscient, omnipresent, and the source of all authority. American scholars were skeptical that German society could ever change.

Another postwar survey of German youths aged fourteen to eighteen found that they presumed American occupation leaders would solve problems in an authoritarian fashion. A majority agreed National Socialism had been a good idea, but it was not properly implemented. While they felt that Germany should become a democracy, many were unclear as to what democracy was. This study also concluded that German authoritarianism was not likely to change.[6]

STEREOTYPES

Also after the war, a German American psychiatrist administered a questionnaire to 2,000 Germans and found they believed in emphasizing discipline in childrearing. Respondents believed that if the child did as told, its world would become simple and rewarding. Children enjoyed following established formulas.[7]

However, caution is in order. Some situations may foster obedience almost regardless of personality. This was demonstrated in the United States by the infamous Milgram experiments. People were told to administer shocks to a "learner" who was actually a stooge. Most people applied "shocks" so severe that they would have been lethal if they were real. The same automatic obedience occurred among college students in the infamous Stanford prison experiment.[8] When the Milgram experiment was repeated in Germany, the same proportion of people obeyed the orders as in America. Obedience can be a response to social pressures rather than a true measure of personality traits. Certainly the Nazis exerted great pressure to obey—and serious, often fatal, consequences for noncompliance. Individuals of most nationalities can obediently respond to authorities, as was also shown in the My Lai massacre by American troops during the Vietnam War.

Questioning Obedience

An American teacher born in Germany, Gerda Lederer, returned there in 1973, hoping to find out why German students were superior to Americans in mathematics.[9] She was shocked when German teachers admonished her not to tell students to be quiet nor impose discipline in the classroom. The aim of the educational system was now to teach students to question the authority of teachers and parents. Many Germans wanted to get away from the habits of obedience that had paved the way for the Nazis and the Holocaust.

Lederer saw that German students were less compliant and more supportive of democratic values than American children of that era. She collected systematic data that validated her observations and found studies from right after the war that confirmed that a change from authoritarian attitudes to democratic ones had developed.

Other studies substantiated what Lederer found. A 1975 study showed German adolescents ranked higher on measures of democratic values and lower on authoritarian values than in all nine other nations studied.[10] A 1980 study showed that Germans had more democratic attitudes than people in Britain and the United States.[11]

Apparently behind the decrease in German authoritarianism were changes in families toward a more egalitarian power structure.[12] Some fathers did not come back from POW camps until as late as ten years after the war. Even when fathers were present, in 49 percent of families the mothers managed family expenses; 27 percent of parents shared money management; and in only 24 percent did fathers supervise the finances. Many fathers had lost their dominant role in the family.[13]

A 2005 study found that many cultural values in Germany were similar to those of the United States in the more liberal era of the 1970s. Germany had decriminalized the consumption, possession, and import of reasonable amounts of drugs like marijuana. By 2005, Americans, more than Germans, espoused conservatism, authoritative rule to maintain morality, and an emphasis on controlling children in educational settings. Life was more liberal in Germany than America. So much for the stereotype of the authoritarian and obedient Germans!

Workaholic Germans

Is German success due to their working harder? Willy Hellpacht, a psychologist, politician, and longtime observer of German character, noted in 1954 that his compatriots had an "urge to work."[14] There is a social obligation to be busy, to be a decent person, and to be a part of German society.

Since the sixteenth century, begging was forbidden for the healthy and able-bodied. Laziness was frowned on, too. If a man was not working at a job, he was expected to be involved in productive tasks, such as house repairs, gardening, or various kinds of self-improvement. It was the duty of citizens to be busy and increase their assets, to add to the collective wealth of the state. Doing anything less was considered a form of early death.

STEREOTYPES

Germans typically have great energy for life. However, one never hears that they are dead tired after working. A 1984 survey found that only 25 percent of Germans agreed with the statement "I always give my best at work, regardless of how much I earn for it." In contrast, 50 percent of Americans agreed with the same statement.[15]

After work, many Germans go bowling, sing in a chorus, take care of the house and garden, take part in church activities, play cards, or go out for drinks, and on Sundays take walks with the family. In my experience, they also are passionate in their discussions about politics. They also often have heartfelt attitudes about truth, beauty, freedom, love, and so on. Perhaps Germans are also energized in these discussions because they seem reluctant to admit being wrong.[16]

In contrast, Americans usually follow the puritanical Calvinist idea that work is a means to an end—at one time salvation, but more recently, success or accumulating wealth. Germans like money, too, but it often has a different meaning for them—they only want enough for security. In America, success often equates to making more money than others, and that is why Americans will work much more than many other people. Americans can become workaholics because achievement is very important for them—not so for Germans.[17,18] A projective psychological test confirmed that Germans have less unconscious need for achievement than Americans.[21]

Research shows that modern German are quite tolerant, permissive, liberal, and rejecting of materialism. Germans expect, and get, ample social welfare. They feel a collective responsibility for the needs of individuals. A national health policy for all citizens has long been accepted as a matter of course.[19]

Today, among the citizens of the member nations of the OECD, Germans work relatively few hours per year, an average of only 1,413, while Americans work 1,787, Canadians 1,702, Swedes 1,644, British,1,625, and the French 1,476. Only the Dutch work less than the Germans, at 1,379 hours per year.

Germans have up to 147 holidays in the year.[16] Furthermore, instead of the customary two weeks of vacation in America, most

Germans have six weeks of vacation. America is clearly a land of workaholics. Americans also retire later than people in much of industrialized Europe, including Germany.

Rather than working more and harder, Germany's workers work smarter. Ever since the late nineteenth century, Germany has emphasized education to create a more productive workforce. About two-thirds of all students graduating from school decide to go into vocational training programs. These consist of two to three-and-a-half years of combined theoretical classroom learning and on-the-job training. Vocational education is not a dumping ground for poorer students, as it was for so many years in America. Those with such technical educations can even go on to lead a company. There are also dual vocational programs that last three to five years and end in a degree. They are especially common in business and engineering. This is not to say that college is neglected. College attendance is very popular, especially since undergraduate tuition is free at Germany's public universities.

Because of the dual educational system of theoretical and on-the-job training in the German apprenticeship system, German workers are flexible. They are not so concerned with protecting specific job duties. This makes labor negotiations more consensus-based and less confrontational than in other countries. Germany lost an average of eleven days of work each year per 1,000 employees due to strikes and lockouts between 1991 and 1999 and only five days per 1,000 employees between 2000 and 2007. These figures compare to forty and thirty-two days in the United States, seventy-three and 103 in France, 158 and ninety-three days in Italy, and 220 and 164 days in Canada.

Perhaps related to working smarter, or at least being more motivated, is the structure of German industry. The *Mittelstand*, the name for small and medium-sized firms, comprises much of industry. These firms are often family owned, with generational continuity and a long-term focus so that workers have an emotional attachment and a willingness to be flexible. Such firms can invest in their workers.

While thoughts of aggression and high achievement have ebbed in Germany, in the twenty-first century Germany has again become powerful. Some other Europeans clearly see Germany as throwing its weight around. Germany's large population, strong economy, and banking prowess have enabled it to control the European Financial Stability Facility, which can disperse money for distressed Eurozone countries. The economic power of Germany and its insistence on austerity measures to solve indebtedness has led newspapers in other countries to portray Chancellor Angela Merkel as a new Hitler. There is even talk of modern Germany being a Fourth Reich.[20]

In subsequent chapters I will detail psychological and cultural factors that play a role in Germany's success, but a very high level of achievement motivation is not one of them.

2: OBJECTIVE DATA ABOUT GERMANS

Three exemplary psychological studies portray Germans in an objective comparative fashion.

An excellent study that avoided simplistic stereotypes surveyed people who had repeated close contact with members of several other nations.[21] Members of the European University Institute typically spend one or more years working as administrators, professors, research assistants, research fellows, and student researchers. They come from England, France, Germany, Italy, and the Netherlands. The investigators in this study administered a questionnaire and, most importantly, conducted long open-ended interviews. (Many other studies obtain only simple answers to closed-ended questions.) The investigators also observed interactions between members of the different national groups.

About 65 percent of the study respondents stated that their ideas on the cultural and psychological differences between nations had become clearer after they had spent time at the institute. They had also become more outspoken about which nationalities they preferred.

All but one of the 100 respondents agreed with the statement: "My nation is characterized by certain distinct traditions," and 93 percent agreed, at least to some extent, that: "The people of my country have certain personality traits which are, on the whole, different from those of people from other countries."

The most common judgment about Germans made by members of the other four nations was that they had a bureaucratic mentality. Almost half of respondents used related terms characterizing Germans as orderly, overly disciplined, overly organized, efficient, rule-obeying, rigid, inflexible, and punctual. These traits are mostly parts of the psychological syndrome of conscientiousness, one of the so-called "Big Five" personality syndromes.[22]

In addition, a quarter of respondents characterized the social style of the Germans as serious, dull, boring, heavy, and lacking a sense of humor. These qualities fall under a couple of other psychological measures covered by the Big Five, agreeableness-disagreeableness and extraversion-introversion.

A fifth of the respondents saw Germans as hardworking, industrious, laborious, and ambitious, living for work and oppressed by work as a duty. These traits are also part of conscientiousness.

Interestingly enough, about a tenth of respondents suggested that the bureaucratic mentality of the Germans was a cover for some irrationality. The Germans, they suggested, were really romantic, sentimental, and empathetic, as well as complex, awkward, and angst-ridden. While the Germans seemed formal and correct, they were really hiding strong emotions, which sometimes came out suddenly. Another Big Five syndrome, neuroticism, covers some of these characteristics. Also, another tenth of respondents saw the Germans as deep, philosophical, or metaphysical, covered by still another syndrome of the Big Five, openness.

Relatively few respondents said they preferred the company of Germans or reported friendly relations with Germans. The Germans were seen as dull and boring. In addition, a tenth saw Germans as intellectually arrogant—they knew better or were convinced they were right. These traits are also connected to introversion and disagreeableness.

Ratings of traits often have a negative bias that enforces stereotypes. An ingenious research study obtained ratings with the evaluative component removed for six different groups, including Germans and Americans.[23] Traits were rated along a positive-to-negative scale, such as thrifty to extravagant. A second scale used similar traits such as stingy to generous. The second scale's values ran in the opposite direction from the first so they could be subtracted from the first scale in order to reduce the evaluative bias often part of ratings.

In this study, Germans were rated as quite different from Americans. They were thrifty, serious, firm, self-controlled, skeptical, persistent, and selective. Americans were seen as more generous, casual, lenient, spontaneous, trusting, flexible, and broad-minded. Significantly, the Germans were the only one of the six national groups in the study to be rated as more "admirable" than "likeable."

A third important psychological study was completely open-ended. The respondents were asked to write personal self-descriptions rather than answering questions of the investigator.

Some of the self-descriptions written included:

—Rather moody, moods can change abruptly from desperately sad to extremely happy and vice versa

—Decidedly labile

—Becomes jittery very easily and excited

—Moods are very diverse, from "sky high" to "mortally grieved" and change very frequently

—Cannot hide bad moods

—From time to time simply can't get rid of certain feelings of distress

—Sometimes too wound up and overexcited

—Often very unstable, moody

Similar self-descriptive statements about emotional instability or changeability came from half of the sixty German respondents. Not a single American respondent made similar statements.

Germans also wrote about the anxious aspect of their inner lives:

—Anxiety states characterize the inner landscape of the soul, afraid of rejection

—A rather anxious person

—Afraid of many things new and unfamiliar

—Afraid of being hurt, being laughed at for doing something wrong

—Being afraid of life

—Observes every little stirring inside, every little pain or whatever; in fantasies they mushroom into incurable illnesses and similar tragedies, into pure and simple anxiety

—Rather afraid of being ostracized

Some of these anxieties were social, being afraid of rejection, being hurt or laughed at—but others seemed to be existential anxieties, such as the fear of being alone over a long time, or *Lebensangst* (life anxiety), or the fear of things new and unfamiliar. Eight of the eleven persons writing about anxiety used the word

Angst. All of these statements came from Germans. Not a single American revealed similar anxieties.

Both the anxieties and instabilities comprised a relatively large proportion of all self-descriptions written by the Germans. Both of these are aspects of the Big Five syndrome of neuroticism, and they are clearly an important part of life for Germans. This was not at all true for Americans.

Angst is one of the most serious forms of German anxiety. It does not refer to a specific fear about something, but a terrible dread about unknown and unknowable matters. It is a very important part of German character. Much of German culture defends against *Angst*—the many rules, the obligations for industriousness and carefulness, the need for complete information, and the adherence to strict time schedules. *Angst* is a key explanation for a host of German phenomena.

The Big Five

The "Big Five" syndromes were developed by psychologists who assembled large lists of personality traits that were associated, then grouped to provide descriptions of different people. Translated lists of these traits have been studied in many countries, and the same five groups have been found to apply to many nationalities.[22, 24]

The first of the five syndromes is extraversion-introversion. Extraverts are talkative, aggressive, verbal, assertive, unrestrained, and outspoken. Introverts are shy, quiet, withdrawn, and inhibited. Germans are more introverted, Americans more extraverted.

A second syndrome is agreeableness-disagreeableness. Agreeable people are sympathetic, kind, warm, understanding, and sincere. Disagreeable people are unsympathetic, unkind, harsh, cruel, and unforgiving. Germans seem to be more disagreeable, Americans more agreeable.

OBJECTIVE DATA

A third syndrome, conscientiousness, is obvious in German personality and culture. Conscientious people are organized, orderly, systematic, efficient, precise, and prompt. A common cliché is that the trains run on time in Germany.

A fourth syndrome, neuroticism, includes negative descriptors such as moody, jealous, and anxious. The anxiety may play a role in fostering the German culture of rules, planning, and expertise.

The fifth syndrome, openness, includes adjectives such as creative, philosophical, and complex. These are traditionally seen as very characteristic of Germans.

3: EXTRAVERSION-INTROVERSION

In the psychological study that asked for self-descriptions, 75 percent of American statements were about what they did well in social situations, while Germans admitted their social strengths and weaknesses only in equal amounts. As other studies have shown, Americans are mostly extraverts, focused on other people. In the self-description study, Americans described themselves as "able to make friends easily," "can make others feel at ease in difficult situations," and "handle myself well in social situations." In contrast, Germans are more likely to be introverts. Some of the Germans admitted they were reserved and often shy.[25]

By and large, the Americans described themselves as friendly or easy to get along with. They saw themselves as relaxed, casual, and accessible when with others. While some Germans described themselves in similar terms, others spoke of themselves as being unsociable, being passive so they could better observe others, needing their own space, and being cautious and wary.

Clearly, Germans and Americans differ greatly on the dimension of extraversion-introversion. These traits were originally described by Carl Jung and have subsequently received a lot of attention from psychologists. An extravert primarily obtains gratification from outside the self. Extraverts tend to enjoy human interactions and to be enthusiastic, talkative, assertive, and gregarious. Extraverts thrive from being around other people. They take pleasure in large social gatherings. Earlier studies of extraversion used the term "surgency" because of the trait's energizing qualities.[26]

In contrast, the introvert is predominantly interested in his or her own mental self. Introverts are typically perceived as reserved or reflective. Some researchers have characterized introverts as people whose energy tends to expand through reflection and dwindle from interaction. One physiological explanation is that introverts have an excess of the neurotransmitter dopamine, and they need time away from people so that their level of dopamine can subside.[27]

Protestantism has been very important in Germany. When

protestant Prussia unified the various German states, Protestantism came to dominate religious life. Protestantism still fosters the individualism of many Germans over more social feelings. An anthropologist studied two adjacent villages that had been either Catholic or Protestant since the Thirty Years' War of the seventeenth century.[28] He observed that when people left church on Sunday in the Catholic village, they greeted one another and talked for quite a while. Then they went in groups to the village inn for more socializing. In the Protestant village, everyone chatted only briefly and then went home. They didn't seem to need the social contacts as much as the Catholics. Generations of life as Protestants, where one didn't need a priest to talk to God, seemed to have fostered a culture of individualism. In fact, research shows that Protestant countries like Germany tend to have more individualistic cultures.[29]

Germans clearly focus more on their individual selves than do Americans. One study found that German high school students emphasized individual activity 50 percent more than they did group activities. In contrast, Americans focused 500 percent more on group activities than on individual activities. The Americans were also much more other-directed, admitting they were influenced by public opinion.

Significantly, researchers have found that introverts learn better when punishments are applied. In contrast, rewards work better for extraverts.[30] There is a great reliance on punishments in German society. Pain can make introverted Germans pay attention, more so than extraverted Americans.

In general, people in countries settled by immigrants, like America and Canada, have been found to be more extraverted compared to people in the sending countries, such as Germany and Ireland. Immigrants are ready to make new lives with other people, including strangers.[31]

Privacy

Eminent German social psychologist Kurt Lewin emigrated to America in the 1930s, and the differences he saw between Germans and Americans impelled him to postulate a German need for privacy. He described the German psyche in terms of layers surrounding the innermost feelings, like an onion. Americans had only a single internal psychic boundary at the deepest layer of the personality. Lewin also suggested that Germans kept more social distance, allowing less accessibility to even peripheral parts of the personality.[32]

Friendships of Germans tend to be close. Quality, not quantity, is important. The research obtaining self-description essays showed that while the American writers highlighted the number of their friends, the Germans emphasized the depth and closeness of their friendships. Germans have fewer but deeper friends, Americans more but shallower friendships. Also, uniquely for the Germans, but not the Americans, was the ability to trust others. However, some Germans also were concerned with being too easily influenced or accommodating, so there can be a certain wariness and caution in dealing with others. They felt ill at ease in some intimate social situations.[25] One interpretation of the German need for privacy is that it is related to their need to control their personal environment.[33]

An anthropologist, Edward Hall, has noted that some Germans feel that it's intrusive to look at other people in public, even from a distance. They also feel strangers shouldn't take photos of others unless they ask permission.[34] In recent times, Germans have become very concerned about Google and other firms that gather personal information on the Internet.

Germans have a strong need to screen their ego from others. Even in Second World War POW camps, Germans built their own tiny shelters to preserve their privacy. In Germany, it is a violation of social mores during an interview to change the position of one's chair and move closer to the other person. Germans are also careful not to touch others accidentally or show intimacy in public.[35]

A guide for American psychotherapists emphasizes that the boundary between the German American family and society is clearly defined.[36] In Germany, politicians generally do not involve their families in public life. The family's life should be protected against intrusions from the outside. Also, German houses are usually surrounded by a fence or bushes, and, even if not fenced, yards are sacred private spaces.[34]

German visitors to America showed their need for privacy while working for IBM. They became upset with the narrow panes of glass in their office doors, whose purpose was for visitors to see if those inside could be disturbed or not. The Germans reacted by hanging their coats over the windows.[37]

Control

Extroverts are uninhibited. Introverts are reserved and guarded, controlling their emotions to maintain predictability and to avoid uncertainties that might trigger anxiety. Emotions can be particularly dangerous in this respect.

The significance of control for Germans was demonstrated in a study of crowded rooms. Individuals with a high need for control perceived the room as more crowded than did subjects scoring low on the desire for control.[33]

A woman with a German background once told me of emotional expression at a funeral. She observed that her German immigrant relatives were stoic, holding in their feelings. In contrast, her husband's American relatives could reveal how much they were hurting. Research shows that Germans especially control expressions of sadness.[38] In the study with unbiased ratings, five other nationalities rated Germans as self-controlled, Americans as spontaneous, Germans serious and Americans lighthearted. Not surprisingly, loneliness was rated positively by the Germans, negatively by Americans.[23, 39, 40]

Research has found German boys agree more than Americans do with the statement "It is better to go without something than to ask a favor" and "If you get bad news, it is better to hide what you feel and behave as if you didn't care."

The study that collected self-descriptive essays found that Americans could write about their aggressive and even hateful feelings, as well as their feelings of envy and jealousy, but Germans couldn't. They bottled feelings up. Some Germans wished that they had even greater control over their feelings.[25]

This study also revealed that Germans could feel depression very

EXTRAVERSION-INTROVERSION

intensely, but they were not likely to express it openly. Generally, German emotional expressions were subdued, in part because they preferred to take a rational, seemingly objective, stance toward life. In addition, Germans do not easily express affection and other emotions.[41] They seem to keep much of what they might experience within strict boundaries. Perhaps the famed German frugality and high savings rate reflect emotional control. However, there is an exception to this holding in of emotions: research has revealed Germans more ready to express anger at violations of norms than Americans.[42]

Of course, Germans aren't always wooden sticks. An acceptable form of overt expression of emotion is *Gemütlichkeit* or geniality and warmth. Such emotions can be expressed when one feels comfortable and experiences familiarity and personal closeness. *Gemütlichkeit* often occurs when Germans are having fun in jovial yet orderly activities. Families in Germany often find *Gemütlichkeit* in their Sunday stroll together, family visits, or while drinking wine or beer with friends.

Freudians have conceptualized impulse control in terms of ego development: not letting impulses of the id get the upper hand.[43,44] Of course, too much impulse control can lead to rigidity, regimentation, compulsiveness, and obsessiveness. These traits sometimes appear in Germans who have suffered severe punishment.

Introversion seems not to have any important direct relationship to Germany's industriousness and economic prowess, except perhaps in the emphasis on manufacturing rather than services. Extroverts thrive in two occupations that involve a high degree of social interaction, sales and management. Other occupations studied, professionals, police, and skilled/semi-skilled workers, did not show any influence on performance by either extraversion or introversion.[45,46]

4: AGREEABLENESS-DISAGREEABLENESS

A typical joke on the Internet illustrates the stereotype of Germans as disagreeable: "Why do they bury Germans sixty feet underground? Because deep down they are really nice."

Willy Hellpacht, psychologist and observer of German mentality, characterized public life in Germany as abrasive and uncivil.[14] Goethe wrote in *Faust*, "If you speak politely in German, you are lying." Eugen Diesel, a writer on German culture and mentality, generalized that "Germans show great patience in their work and in submitting to rules and regulations, but they show little patience in dealing with their fellow-men and the trials of circumstance."[47]

Each of the objective psychological studies introduced earlier confirms that Germans tend towards the Big Five's syndrome of disagreeableness more than agreeableness. The bias-free ratings study found Germans as frank and Americans as tactful and Germans as firm with Americans as lenient. Recall also that the study revealed Germans as the only one of six national groups seen as more admirable than likeable.[23] The European University Institute study similarly revealed Germans as serious, dull, boring, heavy, and lacking a sense of humor. The study that collected self-descriptions found a German preference for being serious, while Americans described that they felt less burdened by life and more carefree.[25]

To be serious is almost a moral requirement for Germans, especially in work, but this is often true at other times, too. Germans must put their whole heart into everything. To say a German is careless or not serious is a major insult. Germans avoid "small talk."

Germans will typically praise someone with the term *solide*—solid, steady, and rational. Humor, especially black humor, is avoided. The study at the European University Institute rated the Germans as humorless. Actually, Germans keep a sharp boundary between joking and earnestness. They won't interject a joke into a serious discussion. They clearly separate work and fun. There is an old German saying: "First work, then play."[48] Even playing cards or bowling can be seen as serious matters.[16]

Managers in a German company, Siemens, prepare their employees for working in the United States by noting how American managers prefer to use the "hamburger" approach to cushion their criticism of subordinates. Americans start with the top of the hamburger bun, the small talk: "How's the family?" Then Americans will slip in the criticism, the meat. Finally they will close with the bottom of the bun, encouraging words. By contrast, in Germany all you get is the meat, the criticism.[37]

Similarly, a research study of 457 middle managers in Germany concluded that they were "tough on the issue, tough on the person." They emphasized performance. Their human relations orientation was low.[49] Much research on group dynamics shows that individuals must often choose between a focus on tasks or on socio-emotional relations. Germans often choose a task emphasis.[50]

The study compiling self-descriptions found that the Germans, in contrast to Americans, were used to getting and giving criticism. In fact, the Germans valued critical comments from others, even if they were painful. Americans invariably indicated that criticism was undesirable, but 71 percent of the German self-descriptions indicated that the expression of critical thoughts and feelings was desirable.[25]

A recent German immigrant to America emphasized to me that Germans like to be direct: "I can still like you even if I don't like your tie. I want to be honest." She explained that Germans feel honesty makes for better relationships. Unfortunately, her direct style makes her seem "unfeminine" to Americans. American men are not used to such frankness, especially from a woman.

Public and Private Behavior

Some people may find this picture of German psychological disagreeableness hard to accept. Germans are known for *Gemütlichkeit*: sentimentality, coziness, well-being, and belonging. But only in certain situations.

German sociologist Ferdinand Tönnies distinguished between two different forms of social relations, *Germeinschaft* and *Gesellschaft*.

AGREEABLENESS-DISAGREEABLENESS

Americans do not clearly separate these private and public spheres of life like Germans and some other peoples do. In *Germeinschaft*, relationships are based on subjective feelings, as in a family or a small community. In more public situations, a *Gesellschaft*, relations are impersonal and rational, more formal, even contractual. Much of German disagreeableness noticed by observers is found in the public sphere, not the private sphere. Of course, there can be exceptions, such as a beer festival, where alcohol dissolves uptight public personas. In contrast, Americans are friendly to strangers most of the time, even without beer.

German has two distinct words for "you": *Du* for informal relationships and *Sie* for formal relationships. People outside the family or a close friendship are referred to with "*Sie*." Because Americans don't make a sharp distinction between public and private spheres, German immigrants often complain that Americans are insincere. Americans say things like, "We will have to get together sometime." But they don't always really mean it.

As mentioned earlier, Germans keep more social distance, or less accessibility, for peripheral parts of the personality in public. They are relatively slow to warm up to others. They're also not quick to express compliments. In Germany, it is assumed that everything is satisfactory unless told otherwise. An immigrant to America told me how pleased she was to get compliments when she met someone. That never seemed to happen in Germany. Americans notice that Germans often do not smile when introduced. Smiling is reserved just for friends.[34]

A German immigrant who had lived for some time in America recalled for me her shock while buying a train ticket in Germany. There was no one else in the line behind her, so she asked the clerk which platform was the right one was for her train. He barked: "information board, over there!" She had forgotten how German officials could be rough and abrupt.

In business, Germans will usually look earnestly for deficiencies in products and will criticize openly if something fails to match claims. Germans try hard not to make mistakes, but if you do, they will be sure to tell you about it. They don't see that as rude, but as part of their need for order.[51]

An American biographer who studied the German playwright Bertolt Brecht during his years in exile in America criticized him as being unfriendly, not willing to socialize. The biographer didn't visit Brecht at home, where he could have seen him having fun with family members.[52] While Germans may often seem disagreeable, in private or in intimate settings they can be warm, friendly, and cheerful.

Lack of Positive Words

A German psychologist has tried to explain modern American positive psychology to German colleagues. He found this movement "un-German," pointing to a lack of positive words in German, especially for emotions.[53] According to philosopher Ludwig Wittgenstein, "The limits of my language mean the limits of my world" and "Whereof one cannot speak, thereof one must be silent."

Not surprisingly, the research study with self-descriptive essays found that Germans described their interpersonal strengths in numbers equal to their weaknesses, while the Americans emphasized their positive strengths over their weaknesses.[25]

One sometimes sees articles by non-Germans on "why I hate Germans" or expressing similar negative views. Germans have recognized their reputation, writing how they are *hässlich*, hated.[54] A 1964 cover article in the newsmagazine *Der Spiegel* dealt with this topic. Another serious publication, *Die Zeit*, carried an article headlined, "The hated Germans are again here." Websites and blogs detail why people hate Germans. A 1991 book, *The Ugly Germans*, has a chapter asking "Can Poles and Germans be friends?"

In one experiment done in France, Spain, Italy, and Germany, the researchers' car purposefully responded slowly when a traffic light turned green. On the rear of their car was an insignia for either Germany or Australia. The waiting motorists from each of the other three nations were all patient when blocked by the Australian car, but they started honking when blocked by the German car.[55]

AGREEABLENESS-DISAGREEABLENESS

A survey just before German unification asked Europeans if they either liked or disliked the Germans. One quarter expressed a dislike of the Germans—this, even forty-five years after the end of the Second World War. When asked if they would be worried by a reunified Germany becoming the dominant power in Europe, half of those surveyed in Great Britain and in France and over two-thirds in Poland said they would be. Common reasons for those worries were that Germany might try to expand its territory again, the German economy might become too strong, or fascism might return. Earlier, in 1977, French people were asked what they thought when they heard the word "Germany," and one third answered "war."[54]

Theodor Heuss, the first president of the German Republic, pointed out that during Napoleon's time the French were condemned as eternal troublemakers. These negative feelings towards the warlike French of that time eventually diminished, so these recently expressed dislikes of the Germans will eventually dissipate, too.[56]

On the other hand, a couple of aspects of German behavior may make it hard to shake the impression of disagreeableness given to others. Work is treated as a serious business by Germans, and much disagreeableness seems due to this emphasis on tasks rather than feelings for the people involved in them. Germans are not pleasant extroverts who make business partners feel warmly toward them. But if Germans were to give up their task orientation, they could become anxious, which might diminish their performance. They also commonly use punishment for teaching, thus also contributing to the impression of disagreeableness. I will discuss this under the Big Five syndrome of neuroticism.

German disagreeableness has failed to show any consistent important relationships to economic performance. Only a few particular occupations show any relationship and the effects are very small. We will see that the next Big Five syndrome, conscientiousness, is the main one with evidence on performance.[46]

5: CONSCIENTIOUSNESS

Of the Big Five Personality syndromes, conscientiousness is probably the most recognizable of German personality characteristics. Many of its traits are aspects of the typical German, who is organized, neat, orderly, systematic, efficient, precise, prompt, exacting, and meticulous. Most can be subsumed under the notion of order, a cardinal aspect of German mentality.

The European University Institute study found that the most common observation about Germans by members of the other four nations was that they had a bureaucratic mentality. The respondents also labeled Germans as orderly, over-disciplined, over-organized, efficient, rule-obeying, rigid, inflexible, and punctual.

The study that collected bias-free ratings from people of different countries also confirmed Germans as high on conscientiousness. The Germans were rated as thrifty, Americans as generous; Germans as persistent and Americans as flexible.[23]

Anal Fixation

Psychoanalysts have long characterized Germans as having an anal fixation. In a 1908 essay, Freud characterized the anal personality as obstinate, orderly, and parsimonious. He claimed that traits such as cleanliness, orderliness, and reliability were related to a repressed interest in unclean things. Freud also cited German folklore, such as the tale of a man who excreted gold coins. The father of Frederick the Great is reported to have negatively responded to a request for money by insisting he had 100,000 men to feed, and he could not shit gold. Postcards of a man shitting money are still popular in today's Germany.

Perhaps the German obsession for cleanliness plays a role in creating an "anal" personality. In Germany, toilet jokes are more popular than the sex jokes common in America. Jokes are often about matters that are anxiety provoking. The American puritanical heritage still operates somewhat in the area of sex. Perhaps German severity in their training for cleanliness plays a role in creating an "anal" personality. In Germany, profanity is usually fecal rather than sexual.[57] A couplet reveals this: *Gut Scheissen das kann sehr beglücken, vielmehr noch als manchmal das Ficken*, "Good shitting, that can make one very happy, much more even than sometimes fucking."

A Freudian folklorist, Alan Dundes, has recounted a history of the German anal fixation back to the time of Martin Luther.[58] Dundes found an inordinate number of German texts concerned with various anal matters: *Scheisse*, or shit; *Dreck*, or dirt; *Mist*, or manure, *Arsch*, or ass, and so on. Dundes titles his book "Life Is Like a Chicken Coop Ladder," after an expression known to many Germans: "Life is like a chicken coop ladder—short and shitty."

An emphasis on the anus pervades German culture. A special issue of *Der Stern* had a forty-page pictorial essay on the history of bathrooms, including discussions of toilet paper and pictures of antique chamber pots. A book by Alfred Limbach was devoted to *Der Furz*, the fart. Many books cite the phrase uttered in Goethe's 1773 play about a renegade knight, Götz von Berlichingen, who said *Leck mich im Asch*, "lick my ass."

Bertolt Brecht's *Baal* and Erich Maria Remarque's *All Quiet on the Western Front* have scatological content. Heinrich Böll's Nobel Prize-winning *Group Portrait with Lady* has a nun at a girl's boarding school who keeps accurate statistical records of 28,000 processes of elimination by the girls.

Martin Luther's inspiration that faith was more important than papal dogma is said to have come to him while he was sitting on the privy. What is more, Luther reported many encounters with the devil who had the face of an anus. Mozart also had an anal fixation. He composed canons for voices repeatedly singing *Leck mich im Arsch*.

Toilet Training

Some Freudians have seen toilet training as fostering German obsessiveness. Toilet training is the first time most children experience parental punishment. Across many cultures, the average time for starting toilet training is roughly twenty-four months, with the American norm closer to eighteen months. One anthropologist's account has German toilet training beginning at about five months, with a belief that the child should be completely "housebroken" by twelve months.[59]

A German immigrant, Sigrid Clark, told me that she was toilet trained at ten months. It wasn't at first successful—the sphincter is not customarily under voluntary control at that time. Clark had to go to a doctor and get shots for her inability to control herself.

A review of criminal abuse of children in Germany found that the most common motive was to enforce toilet training.[60] One researcher saw some changes in German toilet training practices at the end of the 1960s, but a decade later early toilet training was apparently still common.

There is no solid evidence that early severe toilet training fosters obsessiveness or other conscientious personality traits. However, since conscientiousness is important for Germans, causation can run the other way, affecting many things, toilet training and other aspects of childrearing.

Cleanliness is so important in Germany that cleaning is not widely viewed as work. To make something *sauber*, "clean," is an end in itself. "Clean" describes work well done, *saubere Arbeit*, or a nice boy, *sauberen Burschen*, or a good piece of writing, *eine saubere Schrift*. Germans take good care of their forests and fields, their houses and gardens, train stations—they are all *sauber*, in order.

Apparently, it is important to keep the German body *sauber*. A French author noted that the average German uses over three pounds of soap per year, twice as much as a French person. He said Germans use different kinds of soap in the summer and in the winter.[16]

Internal cleanliness is also important. For their health, many Germans take a whole host of tablets and drops. Medical check-ups, the spa or sauna, and fresh air are very important. This emphasis on health extends to what Germans eat. There are thousands of *Reformhäusern*, shops with dietary foods and herbs. Germans are big fans of *Müsli*, *Joghurt*, and *Quark*, healthful foods that are naturally free of contaminants. Beer is consumed in vast quantities, but it should also be pure, brewed only from water, malt, hops, and yeast.

Cleanliness can be pursued to an extreme. Some German householders refuse to use their fireplace because it would create dirty ashes. Germans get their cars washed often. They claim to have invented the car wash.

Order
An anthropologist spent five years doing fieldwork in Germany, and she concluded that "order" was the best single description of German personality and culture. She cited the common German saying, *Ordnung muss sein*—there must be order! People had "a need to straighten things out, to place into categories, to pigeonhole, to strive for precision, to map the territory, to state the boundaries, or to fill in the blanks." In German kindergarten "the children played with neat little toys taken from neat little shelves." The ruling maxim seemed to be "a place for everything and everything in its place." When the children had arts and crafts, the items they produced were cut out from indicated lines and pasted together in prearranged patterns.[61] When she interviewed a social worker concerned with the treatment of disturbed children, she learned that if a child could be classified as having a clearly defined problem, the child could be treated. Otherwise, the child was simply sent home.[62]

German sayings that emphasize the importance of order include "order rules the world," "order is half of life," and "who has no order will have no success."

Unknowns can be burdensome or terrifying for Germans. To live in a world without strict order leads to insecurity and the fear of making errors. Only when everything has its place does angst recede. Near the end of the Second World War, the Nazis warned people that it was either German victory or Russian chaos. The term "chaos" was used to trigger the greatest fear Germans could imagine.

According to Eugen Diesel, the German passion for order is based on deep-rooted insecurity. Since things are never in perfect order, Germans like to get away from the constant pressure to make things better so they travel. Half of all Germans travel to other countries each year. Immersion in another culture is an escape from needing to fix things at home. The aim of German travelling is not

CONSCIENTIOUSNESS

to alter the rest of the world, but to get rid of inner distress.[16] (More about this in Chapter 6)[63]

In general, most Germans accept the creation of order as a daily duty. Germans often look for signs with rules, such as "do not walk on the grass." Order is part of obedience and the acceptance of authority and the security that goes with it.

The emphasis on tidiness and meticulousness can be an indication of respect for things over people.[64, 65] A German American psychoanalyst once told me that Germans tend to cathect, or invest feelings on, things, rather than on people as Americans do. The achievements of Germans in science and technology could well have some basis in their preference for dealing with the greater certainties of inanimate rather than animate objects. German Americans, even in their third generation in America, are still overrepresented in engineering.[66] A focus on things can reduce the uncertainties that are often troubling for Germans.

Efficiency

A German immigrant told me that he left for America because efficiency was worshiped there. He and his wife decided they wouldn't have children because, he said, "Once you have a child, it is like being crippled, with one leg."

At least one management expert considers "efficiency" a dirty world. It usually requires careful measurement, and because costs are typically more easily measured than effectiveness, then goals can be slighted.[68] However, efficiency is an important part of the conscientiousness syndrome. Germans naturally value efficiency, not only in economics but also for other matters, such as the smooth functioning of institutions.[23]

Researchers studied efficiency in different countries by observing the typical speed at which people walked sixty feet, the speed of service by postal clerks, and the accuracy of public clocks. By these measures, Germany ranked third-most efficient, and the United States came in sixteenth.[69] Perhaps the German love of efficiency explains the very high speeds cars travel on the autobahns. Germans hate to waste time. Actually, Germans hate waste of all kinds.

One aspect of efficiency is thriftiness. Germans want to be efficient with their money. The study of bias-free personality ratings clearly showed that stingy Germans are very different from generous Americans.[23]

When German immigrant Heinz Biesdorf joined Cornell University, he developed his Super Shopper Program, which focused on efficiency in shopping. He emphasized grocery shopping since it's done every week, and there are many chances for feedback and learning. An important part of his program was getting to know when items are on sale, then buy in quantity for the home pantry. Biesdorf taught his extension students similar procedures for other kinds of shopping. He developed audio-visual materials for presentations, appeared on radio and television, and was featured in magazines. Biesdorf and his wife were so frugal that when they retired they had to try very hard to spend all their savings.[67]

Punctuality is also an aspect of efficiency. Germans hate to be kept waiting. Because Germans dislike uncertainty, they have a low tolerance if someone can't arrive at a specific time. When a person shows up on time it helps German people trust because they feel more certain about the individual. Arriving a few minutes late will make a bad impression. Schedules are planned to the minute, and meetings are planned far in advance. For Germans, keeping one waiting even a minute can be seen as a deliberate putdown or a signal that the individual is very disorganized. The presence of schedules is an important part of German culture.

Performance

Research shows conscientiousness generally leads to high levels of performance. Dedication to work is related to industriousness and self-control.[70] Researchers have also demonstrated that conscientious people are responsive, orderly, industrious, self-controlled, and proactive: they make focused efforts towards goals and prevent behaviors that might be disruptive.

Conscientiousness correlates with three different motivations for performance. Individuals who set goals, expect to achieve, and feel a personal sense of efficacy are all high performers.[71] Conscientiousness is also related to intrinsic career success (job satisfaction) and extrinsic success (income and occupational status). These positive effects of conscientiousness are found after statistically controlling for general mental ability.[72]

Studies show that this relationship between conscientiousness and high job performance exists in much of Europe and the United States.[73] Orderliness, self-control, hard work, and dependability also are predictors of higher job performance.[74] Numbers of other researchers have also found conscientiousness related to job performance.[75-77]

A study of tens of thousands of workers showed that conscientiousness was consistently related to high performance at sales work, skilled and semi-skilled jobs, and professional jobs.[45, 46] Another study showed conscientiousness was positively related to performance in sales, customer service, management, and both skilled and semi-skilled work.[78]

In an effort to go beyond simple correlations between conscientiousness and performance, researchers gave individuals computational work in a controlled laboratory situation. The work was designed to eliminate the role of such as intelligence, leaving only measures such as concentration, effort, stress management, and perseverance or industriousness. The results demonstrated that conscientiousness affects performance over and above cognitive factors.[79]

Clearly, conscientiousness is a major key to understanding why Germany has been so economically successful.

6: OPENNESS

The Big Five personality syndrome of openness includes traits of being creative, imaginative, philosophical, complex, and artistic. A tenth of the respondents in the European University Institute study found the Germans to be deep, philosophical, or metaphysical.

Inwardness

Historically, Germans have been characterized for their "inwardness": the sense of profound feelings and ideas, as well as sincerity of thought.[80] This contrasts to Americans and other Anglo-Saxon peoples who more often invest energy in practical, action-oriented ideas. Goethe long ago observed how Germans tormented themselves with philosophical problems, while the English showed great practical intelligence and created an empire.[81] Schopenhauer said Germans searched in the clouds for what lay at their feet.[16]

Martin Luther felt that Lutherans should not get involved in external matters such as politics.[82] For a long time, Lutheran Pietism emphasized deep self-examination and communing directly with God. In a sense, the Lutheran religion immunized Germans against the kinds of individual political actions that led to the French Revolution.[83] Lutheranism emphasized private not public virtues.[82]

This emphasis on subjectivity included the German practice of *Bildung*, or self-education, self-formation, and self-improvement. One study showed a greater attention toward the self by Germans, who ranked inner harmony as their second-highest value. For Americans, it was ninth.[84]

Germans seek profound ideas such as beauty, and, as in Goethe's *Faust*, they may strive for absolute truth, such as a comprehension of the universe. This leads to the development of philosophies. Not surprisingly, universities have always been an important part of German society. More books and newspapers are read per capita than in most other countries. The professor is accorded more respect in Germany than in probably any other country in the world.[80, 85]

Eugen Diesel noted: "There is something a little heavy and pedantic and methodical about Germany." Germans often seek information, principles, and rules of conduct, using abstraction and logic. Goethe observed that Germans require a long time to digest any new point of view.

Friedrich Nietzsche noted that the Germans always wanted to know "what is German." Journalist Walter Laquer observed: "Germans seem to feel the shortcomings of their society more acutely than others, they suffer more from abstract and metaphysical pains than other less philosophically minded nations." Laquer added: "Germans have spent more time than any other nation pondering their identity and their destiny. Such preoccupations point to a deep philosophical bent in their mental make-up but also to insecurity."[86]

Despite their claims, Germans are far from rational in everything. They can prioritize the heart over the head in some things, such as the view of their forests as the mystical, mythical, transcendent symbol of Germany. In 1900, a third of German territory was covered with forests. Today, forestland is rarely converted to other uses. In the late twentieth century, Germans were distressed by *Waldsterben*, the unexplained dying of some forests. It was a national crisis.[87-89]

Germans often develop individual standards for behavior. They are not "other-directed" like Americans. An important goal for many individuals is cultivating subjectivity, including personal emotions and ideas.[23] Germans are "inner-directed."[90] The self-description research found that the German focus on how they feel they ought to behave wasn't found in Americans.[25]

Germans can sometimes escape into idealism and crazy ideologies, even follow demagogues like Hitler who emphasized the myths of German origins and greatness.. Perhaps this is a legacy of the earlier period of cultural Romanticism.

Related to this is their morally acclaimed *deutsche Treue*, German faithfulness. When army officers swore their personal allegiance to Hitler, it became extremely difficult to turn against him during the

Second World War. This finally happened in 1944, two years after the war had been clearly lost. Germans proudly spoke of their loyalty to him as *Kadavergehorsam*, "corpse-like obedience." Germans proudly say, "I have my principles."[16]

Germans can go overboard in love. A comparison with Americans surprisingly found that Germans often have a more passionate view of romantic love, though they agree it can cloud one's judgment. They feel romantic love should not be suppressed by social standards of morality. Love also requires total disclosure to the partner. In addition, Germans claim they would disregard economic security in committing to marriage, even though they do not expect love to last forever.[91]

7: NEUROTICISM

A German once told me a story about a motorist who had a flat tire on a back road at night. He had no car jack, so he headed to a house with lights on. The dog started barking. He worried that it might be too late in the evening to bother someone. He worried the resident would be angry and ask "Why don't you carry a jack in your car, like everybody does?" The door opened and a man looked out and asked what the trouble was. The motorist responded: "My neighbor borrowed my jack, and I don't want your damn jack anyway." The story illustrates how Germans worry so much. Neurotics are anxious and unstable.

Anxiety

Sigmund Freud's psychology was based on the study of Germanic patients, and it dealt mostly with the dynamics of anxiety and the defense mechanisms that can protect against it. Structurally, Freud's ego sat on top of the id with its biological urges. The ego controlled the expression of feelings. At the apex of the personality, Freud put the superego—that is, the conscience, permitting only what parents had encouraged.

Surveys have revealed that anxieties are common in Germany. Anxieties connected to achievement and social situations have been found in 34 percent of the population, panic attacks and phobias in 24 percent, and uncontrollable worries in 20 percent. Over a lifetime, these rates were estimated to be twice as high.[92]

A host of German followers of Freud expanded his emphasis on anxiety. Karen Horney wrote of *The Neurotic Personality of Our Time*, Alfred Adler wrote about inferiority feelings, while Erich Fromm reported how the Germans turned to Hitler and the Nazis in an *Escape from Freedom*. Neo-Freudian Erik Erikson felt that Nazism's success was built on the party's ability to generate attitudes and symbols responding to the crisis in German society after the First World War and, most of all, the presentation of Hitler as the solution to the widespread anxieties of the time.

Recent physiological research has helped elucidate the mechanisms of anxiety.[93] The behavioral activation system (BAS) includes brain regions that regulate arousal, and this system is responsive to rewards. Extroverts with a very active BAS can be impulsive and have difficulty inhibiting behavior when approaching a goal. The fight-flight-freeze-system (FFFS) governs reactions to aversive or punishing stimuli, regulates avoidance behavior, and underlies fear.

The behavioral inhibition system (BIS) mediates conflict between the FFFS (avoidance) and BAS (approach). Conflicts between those two systems underlie anxiety.[94] This research shows fear and anxiety are separate emotions. It's also argued that the BIS reflects, at least partially, effortful control or constraint as a function of the neurotransmitter serotonin.[95]

Earlier research found that anxious people consistently score high in traits of neuroticism and are more introverted than extroverted.[96] They are said to have "trait anxiety." Such people seemed to be physiologically more sensitive to pain or punishment.[30] They also dwell on the negative aspects of the world.

Strange Situation

German anxieties can start early in life. Researchers have observed infants for their reactions to the so-called "Strange Situation," the disappearance and then reappearance of their mother. In the United States, the majority of children seek comforting when the mother reappears, while a few show insecure attachment to the mother by turning away, avoiding, or ignoring her.[97] But in Germany the majority of children were avoidant and insecure, apparently because German mothers seemed to be less tender, less careful, and less affectionate while holding the infants in their arms. The researchers speculated that cultural values in Germany mandated keeping a larger interpersonal distance. German culture required that a baby move on its own sooner. The mother responding to the infant's every cry by picking it up was considered spoiling it. The ideal was an independent, non-clinging infant that does not make demands on the parents but rather unquestioningly obeys their commands.[98, 99] Subsequent separation anxiety was additionally fostered by the insensitivity of mothers—the inability to respond promptly to the child's social gestures, expressions, and signals and avoiding intrusiveness or imposing the mother's agenda on the child, all of which is necessary to show positive feeling towards the child.[104,106] The researchers also found that when an infant was distressed, a father inevitably handed it to the mother.[100]

Researchers have also found that sixteen-year-olds who had tested as insecure as infants in relation to parents showed more disruptive behavior towards a friend in a problem-solving situation.[101] Later research has shown that children observed as insecure in the "strange situation" reveal evidence of insecurity at age nineteen.[102] "Terror management" research (to be discussed below) shows insecure children later focus on adhering to cultural norms in order to dissolve anxiety.

Instability

The postwar Italian writer, Luigi Barzini, issued a book characterizing the essence of each European nation. He saw Germans as "mutable" or changeable.[103] Willy Hellpach referred to "volatile German stubbornness."[14]

Germans often seem to have an inordinate amount of striving, but once a goal is reached, they retain a sense that something more should be done to assure everything is right. Germans can vacillate between hope and fear, between euphoria and apathy or depression, sometimes over a seemingly minor matter. This situation is where German emotional mutability can come to the fore.[16]

This kind of instability has been conceptualized by German American social psychologist Kurt Lewin as a "quasi-stationary equilibrium." He noted that people who are caught between pressures to do or not do something will often make abrupt changes in their behavior if some minor thing is introduced to disturb the equilibrium.[104]

In the self-description research, some of the most striking German accounts involved internal psychological matters, such as being emotionally labile and ridden with both social and existential anxieties. The Germans also described feelings of moodiness and numerous social anxieties with abrupt and tumultuous mood swings and fears of rejection or being ostracized. These issues did not appear at all in the American self-descriptive essays.[25]

In 1931, Eugen Diesel observed that Germans "possess a very definite element of nervous excitability in their disposition" and "a lack of inner poise." Germans didn't seem relaxed. He noted as a symptom of this inner insecurity that simple remarks and observations were often taken wrongly. Furthermore, "Their gestures—for instance the way they are always passing their hands over their forehead or through their hair–give sure proof of this inner restlessness." He added that Germans seemed to be readily moved to hope and enthusiasm, to be easily flattered and easily insulted, and "in general the German lacks inner stability and confidence in himself."

Diesel noted an ever-impending "atmosphere of stifling gloom, the lack of any inner stability and cohesion. The tragic epic of life is played against a chaotic, incoherent background, lacking all unity and compactness." He added that this inner insecurity could be hidden and disguised by professional dignity and an artificial veneer of self-assurance."

Research shows that discrepancies between one's self-image and one's duty or obligation can result in agitation and nervousness.[105] Duty and obligations are very important for Germans, so agitation and nervousness can be common. Discrepancies between ideals, wishes, and hopes and actual situations will trigger dejection or sadness.

Walter Laquer, writing about Germany in the 1980s, noted "there is still, or again, a palpable restlessness, a specific German unease disregarding reality and nurturing illusions about the perfectibility of institutions."[86] He added that since Germans were perfectionists who need order, if things became a little chaotic, if full success were out of reach, there was an all-pervasive fear, a free-floating anxiety, and an assumption that everything that could go wrong would go wrong.

Laquer noted that some Germans even persuaded themselves that only Germany would be destroyed in a nuclear war, while the rest of the world would somehow survive. He added, "There seems to be an inclination to expect the worst among this unquiet people…deep down there still seem to be the same old anxieties, the intensity, the fear of failure, with inability to relax, the difficulty of keeping things in proportion. This is the kind of mental attitude in which molehills become mountains."

On the surface, the average German doesn't seem anxious. Germans are busy and purposeful people, striving to achieve their ambitions. However, many Germans report problems sleeping, waking up in a cold sweat, and worrying. Others report childhood trauma and turmoil that continue to affect them. They have anxieties that are not completely submerged. Much of their behavior has to do with dealing with anxieties so that they no longer show. In fact, Germans buy lots of insurance, they save their money "for a rainy day," and they follow rules in order to avoid surprises.

Punishment

Perhaps the biggest source of German anxieties is the use of punishments that are so effective on introverted Germans. A study confirmed that children who were introverts learned better when teachers used punishments, while rewards worked better for the extraverts.[30]

Study of German child care and youth guidance literature reveals a long tradition of severity, emphasizing that character education must begin in earliest infancy and continue through childhood. Obedience and punishment were emphasized. If the child is left to itself at any point, the child almost invariably will make the wrong choice, do the wrong thing.

In a 1952 study, ten- and eleven-year olds were given stories about a loss or accidental damage for which they had to propose a solution. In the "Lost Cap," Peter and Franz are going to school. Franz grabs Peter's hat and throws it onto a tree. Other stories involved lost sausages, lost money, an ink spot on mother's new coat, a broken window, and a lost composition book. The usual solution proposed by the children was punishment, whether it was a deliberate misdeed or an accident. Punishment was inescapable if the culprit were discovered. No wonder German adults can cite an Eleventh Commandment: Don't Get Caught. Another feature of the children's stories was that punishment might continue as more adults are told of the misdeeds. Mother tells father, or teacher tells principal who also tells the mother, and so on.[106]

A 1974 study observed playgrounds in Germany, Italy, and Denmark. German adults were more aggressive towards their children than parents in the other two countries, and their children were more aggressive towards one another. For example, a child might intentionally ride a bicycle over a sandcastle being built by another. If the child consequently cried, the mother would scream, "Will you stop crying like a baby, or we'll go home." A survey in Germany at that time showed that nearly 60 percent of parents believed in beating their children. A Munich psychologist noted, "We beat our children dumb in this nation."[107]

A researcher has noted that "nowhere in Western Europe are the needs of children so fatally neglected as in Germany." He felt that *Kinderfeindlichkeit* (literally children as enemies or hatred of children) was part of a general German hostility towards "all human beings."[60] Physical punishment of children was eventually made illegal in Germany in 2000. However, a 2012 survey reported that four out of ten parents admitted to smacking their children on their bottoms, and 10 percent to hitting them on the head.[108]

A Variety of Punishments

Physical punishments are the least of the problems children may face in Germany. An immigrant to America told me her father never hit her. He simply used threats, *Du kriegst gleich eine Ohrfeige*, roughly, in a minute I'm going to hit you on the head! Because he hollered at her, she believed him.

In 1845 Dr. Heinrich Hoffmann wrote and illustrated a book, *Der Struwwelpeter*, as a Christmas present for his children. It is a compilation of morality tales in which children are humiliated and mutilated for being stupid or disobedient. Frederick is mean— whipping, kicking, and beating a dog—but it then bites him. Polly plays with matches, her dress catches on fire, and she burns up, leaving only her shoes. Mother tells little Conrad not to suck his thumbs or else the tailor will come and shear them off, but he disobeys and the tailor comes. Casper refuses to eat his soup, and after five days he is dead. Robert refuses to stay inside when a storm comes, so the wind catches his umbrella and he is blown away. The book is still popular in Germany.[109]

St. Nikolas comes to Catholics on December 6 bearing gifts. He is accompanied by Krampus in rough clothes and a hideous mask. One German immigrant recalled for me how Krampus would rattle chains, shake his birch switch, and threaten to take him away in his large sack because he had been bad. He cowered under a table and wet his pants.[110]

Psychoanalyst Alice Miller, writing in the late twentieth century, described two centuries of German child-rearing literature. Some of the "poisonous pedagogy" found by Miller included: obedience makes a child strong; a high degree of self-esteem and tenderness is harmful; severity and coldness are a good preparation for life; parents are always right. Furthermore, it's never too early to teach obedience, since children "will never remember afterwards that they had a will, and for this very reason the severity that is required will not have any serious consequences." A German immigrant told me her father made a special point to abuse her in order to break her will. This was only revealed to her later by her older sister.

According to Miller, children do not later recall the abuse they suffer; they repress such experiences to avoid unbearable pain. Instead, they idealize the parents. The title of one of Miller's books is *Thou Shalt Not Be Aware: Society's Betrayal of the Child*. Miller said the admonishment to honor one's parents was generally followed because those abused were unwilling to testify against parents. Children were expected and commanded to respect and love their abusers because the abuse was "for their own good."[111]

Miller also exposed the all-too-common sexual abuse of girls by fathers. Freud had earlier diagnosed such women as hysterics with fantasies of wanting sex with their fathers. Sadly, such sexual abuse probably still happens.

Miller conducted extensive research on Hitler's early life. Beatings and humiliations began when he was four years old. His father was meting out punishments that he had suffered as a child. Such child abuse was common in Germany during the latter part of the nineteenth century, but not elsewhere. In Prussia and Saxony the number of childhood suicides was three to five times higher than in Sweden, Belgium, France, Austria, Italy, and England.[60]

Psychological Abuse

Miller also cited the common use of humiliation and shaming. Immigrant Sigrid Clark told me that when she returned to Germany for a year of high school, she was appalled by the teachers' frequent use of shame. Earlier in elementary school, she had seen students made to sit in the corner with a dunce cap. In her German high school, each student's grades were announced to the whole class. Clark was continually disparaged by her teacher in front of the class. These experiences brought back for her the horror of growing up and hearing her mother continually say, *schäme Dich*: "you should be ashamed." She remembers doing childish things such as scratching her behind while out on the street, and being rebuked, "What will the neighbors think?"

The use of shame and guilt and the resultant pain and anxieties may account for the relentless quality found in some Germans. They can be driven by an anxiety that they will be punished if things are not done right. Their superego tells them, "Do it or else!"

Clark told me that she was never physically punished as a child; her mother used shame and guilt. Clark became "regimented." She had a feeling about what her mother wanted, and she just "had to do it." Cleaning the stairs "had to be done every Saturday, using steel wool and on your knees, whether the stairs were dirty or not. This feeling sticks with you. Growing up, you learn you have certain tasks that have to be done at certain times, no matter what."

Such compulsiveness seems to have origins in the anxiety resulting from strict punishment. The study with bias-free ratings found that Germans were "persistent" while Americans were "flexible."[23]

A sociologist has theorized that Germany's loss in the First World War triggered enormous shame that helped foster the rise of the Nazis. Previously, Germans had been very proud of their country and its achievements. Then the Versailles Treaty placed the blame for the war on the Germans, exacted punishing reparations, and led to the victors' occupation of German territory. All that was a complete humiliation. Hitler recognized the pain from that shame and used it to gain power over the German people.[112, 113]

Need for Punishments
One psychologist has argued that the very young child has to learn from simple conditioning, without thinking matters through. Parents need to create a negative feeling that running out into the street is undesirable. The child has to associate unpleasant feelings with bad behavior, so that the avoidance response is automatic. When the child is three or older, verbal explanations and rationales can be understood and added.[114, 115]

Why not use just explanations and rewards for good behavior as in the American approach to childrearing?[116, 117] One reason is that many negative actions, such as stealing, lead to an immediate pleasant reward, while the rewards for ethical behavior may be modest or delayed. Negative feelings can be important deterrents. Anxieties persist but rewards fade.[115, 118]

Germans pride themselves on their morality, particularly honesty.[119] In research from the General Social Survey in the United States, German Americans rank honesty higher than do other Americans in the list of values they want to instill in their children. If honesty were taught mainly with rewards it would become part of the positive self, but it also could be relatively flexible. If only punishment were used to create a sense of honesty, it may become an inflexible standard, based more on the letter than the spirit of the law. If some punishment is combined with reward, the anxiety may be covered over, but it is still there, deep down, to motivate honesty.[120, 121] If one starts to succumb as a result of temptation after years of abstinence, the anxiety can again rear up. It is as if anxiety is an internal watchdog. A good example is former President Jimmy Carter who admitted in his famous *Playboy* interview that he was still, despite being born again, on guard against lust in his heart.

Avoiding Risk
Anxious people focus on bad things that can happen. A German immigrant told me how she felt when her adult son said he wanted to bike alone across America. She kept thinking of things that could

go wrong. She'd ask where his packs would be put while shopping at a store. The parent admitted, "Other people might tell their children that it was a great idea, that it'd be a wonderful experience. I thought of things that could go wrong."

German immigrants to America generally shunned risk. One of the reasons Germans are still overrepresented in farming today is the secure living it once provided. Owning a farm meant you were sure to have work, shelter, and food.[122] American farmers with a German heritage also tend to raise a variety of crops and animals, rather than specializing which can be more lucrative but is riskier.[123] As one German farmer told me, when you grow a number of different crops and raise different kinds of animals, no matter what the weather and the markets are, you can usually count on something doing well.[124]

German American farmers have avoided risk in other ways. A banker in a farming community in Nebraska told me how German American farmers were more cautious than non-Germans in asking for a loan. A Michigan farmer told me that his German American neighbors didn't buy the newest, biggest tractor or combine—the investment might not pay off Even after four or five generations in the United States, these descendants of immigrants were generally frugal and cautious.

Perfectionism

The study with bias-free ratings found that Germans were "selective" and Americans "broadminded."[23] Germans often get anxious and upset if things are not as they expect—if the seasoning in the soup tastes a little off, or if two adjoining sheets of wallpaper don't match to within a thirty-second of an inch. Everything has to be in place and coordinated.[125] A typical German advertisement has tennis champion Roger Federer saying that, like tennis stars, coffee machines must be perfect.

Many Germans avoid the uncertainty that goes with having children, who can interfere with a structured existence. Germany has one of the lowest birthrates in Europe.

Research shows that perfectionism is correlated with trait anxiety, the combination of neuroticism and introversion.[126]

Perfectionism and the resultant self-criticism seem common in Germany. According to American psychotherapist David Burns, these traits are perpetuated by perfectionist parents who react to a child's mistakes and failures with anxiety, disappointment, and perhaps punishment. These parents feel their child's shortcomings reflect on them. The child experiences the parents' discomfort as rejection and comes to base self-esteem on getting approval from parents. Often, risky situations are avoided, and the child chooses safer and easier tasks that can be done perfectly.[127]

Negativism and Criticism

Research shows that people with high levels of anxiety have negative thoughts.[128] The self-descriptive research showed Germans recounting their interpersonal strengths as equal in number to their weaknesses. In comparison, Americans emphasized strengths much more than their weaknesses.[25]

Ann Hertz, a German immigrant, told me her father "never, never, ever once praised. I was never good enough for him. I didn't expect him to say, 'I'm proud of you', but at least to say, 'good for you, you made it.' I got so angry. I just had to tell myself it doesn't matter anymore. I'm an adult now." Her father never said anything positive to her mother, either.

The child of a 1930s German refugee told me how her mother's negativity harmed her self-image. Her mother called her a dumb cow, an imbecile. "Sometimes she'd get really angry and say every single thing about me was bad. My mother was always pointing out the things I did wrong. She didn't tell me when I was good. The only way I could think of myself as good was when I didn't do bad things. Sometimes I felt so hopeless. My reaction to my mother was to be the obedient child, I accepted my mother's control. So I never took the initiative in things, and I'm still very shy to this day. My sister rebelled. She disobeyed and went out with Catholic boys, and she eventually married one."

Abuse can lead to low self-esteem.[129, 130] After hearing over and over again that they are dumb, stupid, or clumsy, children can grow up to have social anxieties, fearful of being judged by others. If they don't become very vulnerable to criticism, they can become very angry—or both. They can feel victimized and resentful.

Stress

Germans have a word to describe being overcome with the pressure to always be busy: *Weltschmerz*, or the pain of living. A German immigrant told me how her relatives in Germany, in contrast to Americans, often talk about *Lebensangst*, existence anxiety. Germans can sometimes complain of bad luck or other excuses, but this can be a form of depression, they can blame themselves.[16]

A contractor named Schmidt told me that as a young man in Germany, he vowed he would become a millionaire to prove himself better than his father, who couldn't afford a couple beers at the inn. In America, Schmidt worked long hours, even on weekends. He worshipped efficiency, avoiding waste. Mornings before work, he planned exactly the work his employees would do that day. But even though Schmidt had no financial or business worries, he didn't sleep well and often broke out in cold sweats. He developed a variety of ailments, but his doctor could find nothing physically wrong and suggested he seek treatment for mental problems.

Schmidt finally realized he felt pressure from his workers. He paid them better than anyone else did, but they still wanted more. He explained, "I have this trouble: I keep thinking about something that I want to be right. I don't know what the answer is, but then I keep thinking about other things that are important.

Such job-related stress on the job is common in Germany. A 2012 survey noted the prevalence of early retirement due to psychological problems.[131] But those who surmount such pressures can succeed. One German immigrant, a multi-millionaire, told me he followed his parents' advice: *Gib mal Mühe*—take pains, try harder. This drive to overcome may play an important role in German achievements but also cause others to dislike Germans.

Hypochondria

Because Germans are perfectionists who need order, when things become a little chaotic and full success is out of reach, hypochondria can set in. Walter Laqueur got the impression from

NEUROTICISM

visiting Germany that there was a relatively high level of sensitivity to threatening body sensations.[86, 132, 133] Research confirms the association of trait anxiety with various problems such as premenstrual syndrome, poor cognitive coping, and more difficult delivery of first babies.[134-137]

My German cousin's husband often felt sick when he sat at dinner, and he also slept poorly. He hired a water dowser, who said there was an underground stream that passed under the house under his dining room chair and his side of the bed. The dowser then buried a small gadget to prevent the stream from emitting its damaging rays. My cousin's husband, an elementary school principal, believed in the cure. The dowser had already helped a neighbor, and German television had broadcast programs on the dangers of radiation from underground streams.

Germans often go to spas and bathe in special mineral waters. The German national health service considers a physician's prescription for a stay at a spa as a legitimate cure for "stress." The great number of advertisements for various health potions in Germany also suggests a high rate of hypochondria.

Sensitivity

Neurotic instability and introversion can cause extreme sensitivity to negative stimuli.[96] Introverts notice, learn about, and recall painful stimuli. They seem to have lower sensory thresholds. In contrast, extraverts are more sensitive to rewards. A German immigrant supervisor at an American tool-and-die shop told me about his predominantly German immigrant workforce. Since they were quite sensitive, he made a special effort to say "hello" and "good morning" to everyone. If he forgot anyone, they could feel slighted. The supervisor added, "The Heinies are very sensitive, you know."

Germans are sensitive to negative environmental stimuli. They often have local regulations or informal norms prohibiting excessive noise in restricted hours—even the existence of norms against flushing your toilet in an apartment building late at night. If a large delivery truck does not finish unloading by Saturday evening, it has to remain in the village till Monday morning. In some places in Germany, people have complained about children in playgrounds disturbing the peace.[138]

A psychological experiment might explain Germans' concern about noise. Students were exposed to noises while they had to learn some material. Those high in trait anxiety were not able to recall the material as well as those who were extroverted and not neurotic.[139]

Study of five European nations revealed Germans as the most concerned about environmental issues. In Germany, the Green Party was initially established to deal with pollutants, including automotive emissions and chemicals in streams.

Similarly, one of the stumbling blocks to unification in Europe was a German concern about "pollution" in food. Germany had long strictly limited the ingredients if beer were to be sold as "pure." Otherwise it couldn't be sold as "beer."

Germany scheduled the closure or all its nuclear power plants, because of concerns about radiation. France gets 75 percent of its electricity from nuclear power, and American nuclear plants also remain open.

Angst

Respondents in the University Institute Study characterized the Germans as "angst-ridden." In English, angst usually means anxiety. To Germans it is an anguished terror. Freud differentiated *Realangst*, worry about an identifiable thing, and *neurotische Angst*, anxiety about the unknown.[140]

Angst is a form of indeterminate anxiety about widespread and unknown danger that can't be escaped.[142] The German philosopher Martin Heidegger wrote of *Angst* as an existential threat, a sense that unknowable bad things could happen. Heidegger saw *Angst* arising from the nature of the human condition, not from the fear of any identifiable thing.

Other existential philosophers have written about facing mortality without comforting religious myths. Jean Paul Sartre, who was raised by his German mother and uncle, wrote *Being and Nothingness*. German American theologian Paul Tillich similarly saw *Angst* as the awareness of being finite and threatened by non-being. It was an inescapable part of human freedom. In the study that obtained written self-descriptions, the Germans frequently wrote of their broad existential anxieties.[25]

Germans much more commonly use *Angst* than the word for fear, *Furcht*. Germans say, *Ich habe Angst*, I have a bad feeling without a specific cause. *Angst* is a state, like depression. When Germans use *Furcht*, they will usually specify what thing they fear. The verb *furchten* must have an object. Fear and anxiety are separate emotions—they trigger different parts of the brain.[141] Not knowing what will happen arouses much more anxiety than a real danger, and *Angst* is all about the condition of those who experience it.[16]

According to a frequency dictionary of spoken German, *Angst* occurs fifty-two times in half a million words, while the verb "fear" appears only four times, and the noun "fear" not once. In other languages, speakers do not use terms roughly similar to *Angst* and *Furcht* in these very uneven proportions—except in places like Scandinavia that are predominately Lutheran.[142]

Luther

The word *Angst* appeared in Germany during Martin Luther's life. He translated the Bible into German and wrote many popular religious pieces about the terror of the imminent Judgment Day. Luther also wrote of his great terror of the Devil and was very concerned about going to hell for his sins. One writer at that time observed that "in no country of the world does the devil exercise a more tyrannical power than in Germany." The legend of Faust, who sells his soul to the devil, became a central part of German culture.[16] Luther's writings made *Angst* gain wide currency among Germans.[16]

According to psychoanalyst Erich Fromm, the key to Luther's personality was his *Angst* and his search for a remedy for it. Fellow Lutheran reformer Philip Melanchthon wrote about Luther: "Often, when he was thinking attentively about the wrath of God, or about some startling examples of divine punishment, he would be suddenly struck by such terror as to almost lose consciousness." Luther often thought of suicide. He wasn't just fearing the afterlife; he suffered hellish anguish on earth, feeling God's wrath and rejection.[143]

Luther's theology emphasized that only faith in God, not good works, could bring salvation. According to Fromm, Luther and other reformers gave many people a new feeling of freedom and independence from the Catholic hierarchy of authority. At the same time, the more direct relationship with God meant a feeling of powerlessness and *Angst*. People felt alone and anxious. Fromm wrote of the German need to escape from freedom.

Modern Angst
Research in Germany about the future reveals a diffuse *Angst*. A survey question in 2013 asked: "Do we live today in a particularly insecure time, that is, compared to earlier, one can't calculate or plan less, or would you say that 20 or 30 years ago everything was just as insecure?" Of Germans who were surveyed, 58 percent agreed that the present was particularly insecure, up from 48 percent in 2012 and 44 percent in 2001. When asked to list their worries, 82 percent identified increasing violence and criminality, 74 percent the fear of a terrorist attack in Germany, 73 percent worried that more refugees would come to Germany, 67 percent feared a military conflict, 59 percent worried that their pensions were not secure, and 55 percent that taxes and expenses would rise.

In 2014 through 2016, surveys asked: "Many people have, to be sure, *Angst* that something can happen, one could be a victim of a terrorist attack. How much do you feel threatened by terrorism?" In 2014, 45 percent said they felt "very" or "somewhat" threatened, and that rose to 51 percent in 2015 and 2016.

This pessimism has been long-standing. Surveys in 1967, 1972, and 1975 showed about half of Germans felt that life would not get better in the future. Surveys in 1977, 1978, 1980, and 1982 showed the number saying things would get better fell from 39 percent to 28 percent.[144]

In 1998, Germans had the most pessimistic outlook on life for the coming year, compared to people in the other nations in the European Union. While Germans were fifth-highest in their optimism about general economic prospects for the coming year, they were the most pessimistic of all the nations about their personal finances. Germans were about average in their feelings about the nation's general employment situation but most pessimistic about their personal job situation. In general, Germans thought their country would be OK but felt bad things would happen to them personally. That persisted in surveys done in 2001, 2002, 2003, and 2004.

In 2009, respondents were asked to imagine the European Union twenty years in the future and to compare it with the present. On average, 28 percent of the citizens surveyed in the European Union nations said life would be easier, but only 18 percent of Germans. When asked about the social welfare system in twenty years, 36 percent of all nationalities predicted the coverage would be wide enough, but only 31 percent of Germans agreed.. Germans were consistently more pessimistic than the average European.

In 2010, respondents were asked to rate their current household financial and employment situations, and Germans were more positive than the average European. However, when asked to predict for the coming year, Germans were more negative—and remained that way in surveys from 2012 to 2016.

In 2014 Germans had greater concerns than the average European about someone misusing personal data, the security of online payments, and receiving goods or services bought online. Germans expressed more concerns than the average European about the privacy of the Internet and phones in a 2016 survey. Interviews in 2010 revealed that more Germans also saw negative effects in the next twenty years from biotechnology and genetic engineering than the average European. Germans seemed to be anxious about the future for almost everything!

Like other qualities of German character, *Angst* can become excessive. In 1918, the historian Oswald Spengler writing in *The Decline of the West* saw nothing but bad times ahead for Germany. Perhaps their *Angst* makes Germans excessively sentimental at times like birthdays and makes them prodigious drinkers as means of defending against general melancholy. In fact, their seriousness, their industry, their need for order, and all the other aspects of conscientiousness can also be seen as defenses against *Angst*.[16]

In discussing stereotypes, I have suggested that Germans are no more aggressive than Americans—and maybe less so. However, individual Germans can be assertive and this may be effective in overcoming neurotic fear.[145] Not surprisingly, psychologists suggest that people high in neuroticism may also have a high degree of anger.[146]

Positive Anxiety

Anxieties can supply pressure to enhance performance.[147] A number of psychologists even see genius as flowing from basic anxieties acquired in childhood, perhaps a parent dying or experiences such as abuse and rejection. Psychologist Frank Baron has reported how creative writers often suffer from unresolved anxieties that drive them to produce.[148] Such people seem to have a drive to master, to control, and to push ahead, rather than being swallowed up by anxiety. The anxieties are not often freely admitted, since others may view them as a sign of weakness. This background may come to light later, when the stigma is no longer so damaging, as for example, in the case of the late Petra Kelly, founder of the Green Party in Germany, who was quite anxious as a child. She went on to major achievements before her untimely death.[149]

I've described neuroticism and anxiety and a whole host of its related symptoms such as instability, perfectionism, hypochondria, and sensitivity. For some people, heightened self-control can serve an alternative to expressing the neurotic symptoms examined in this chapter. Conscientiousness in the form of psychological tightness, rather than looseness, can help.[23] Neurotic individuals high on conscientiousness may be able to channel their anxiety so they are motivated to work harder, prepare better, and be more meticulous. A study of anxiety due to job insecurity showed that under some conditions productivity could increase. The more insecurity, the more motivation to produce, although with adverse effects on creativity.[150, 151]

The next section of the book will examine culture. This is especially important because study shows that countries with neurotic personalities are also countries, like Germany, that are characterized by cultures of uncertainty avoidance, and this in turn can foster some elements of conscientiousness, such as being organized and being systematic.

8: CULTURES

An old joke steeped in stereotypes imagines two men and one woman of different nationalities on a desert island. After a month of being stranded there, one of the Italian men had killed the other over the Italian woman, the two Englishmen were still waiting to be introduced to the Englishwoman, the two Japanese men had contacted Tokyo for instructions—and the two German men were following a strict weekly schedule for sharing the German woman. Germans dislike uncertainty; they use rules to solve conflicts.[152]

Culture, in the view of social science, is composed of all the shared customs, behaviors, beliefs, and values transmitted from one generation to the next. Personality and culture reinforce each other. Over time, individual behavior can modify and mold culture so that it becomes relatively congruent with the most typical personalities. At the same time, personalities are molded by childrearing and normative pressures, so that people come to want to do what the culture says they should do.

Uncertainty Avoidance

In 1980 Geert Hofstede published the results of a major study in his book, *Culture's Consequences: International Differences in Work-Related Values*. He surveyed more than 100,000 IBM employees in forty countries. Using factor analysis, he grouped together associated survey responses to construct four basic cultural dimensions: individualism-collectivism, power difference, masculinity, and uncertainty avoidance. Germany and the United States differed most significantly on the last scale.

Hofstede's uncertainty avoidance index for each country was based on three questions that were closely correlated: stress, as expressed in the answer to the question "How often do you feel nervous or tense at work?"; employment stability, based on how long employees intended to continue with the company; and rule orientation, measured by agreement with the statement "Company rules should not be broken—even when the employee thinks it is in the company's best interest." Of these three indicators, "stress" reflects an individual's anxiety over uncertainty. Employment stability and rule orientation can be viewed as coping mechanisms for reducing stress. Germany scored 65 for Uncertainty Avoidance while the United States scored a relatively low 46.

Entropy is a term derived from thermodynamics and information theory to conceptualize how self-organizing systems can lose energy needed to perform work. Individuals and organizations try to maintain order.[153] To do so, they require a modicum of conscientious behavior, organization, systemizing, meticulousness, and precision. Avoidance of uncertainty promotes more efficient work.

Another study of cultural uncertainty avoidance measured agreement with four items:

1. Most organizations would be better off if conflict would be eliminated forever.

2. It is important for a manager to have at hand precise answers to most of the questions that his subordinates may raise about their work.

3. In order to have efficient work relationships, it is often necessary to bypass the hierarchical line. (This item was scored negatively.)

4. An organizational structure in which certain subordinates have two direct bosses should be avoided at all costs.

Of the ten countries studied, the United States scored as the most accepting of uncertainty, while Germany, in contrast, was the fourth highest in avoidance of uncertainty.[154]

In Germany, banking is seen as a very important enterprise. Germans cope with uncertainty by looking for predictability, and bank deposits provide stable investment returns. In the United States, where uncertainty avoidance is low, people accept the unpredictability of stock markets in exchange for the possibility of higher returns. Also, Americans enjoy gambling, which is uncommon in Germany.

Another facet of the German avoidance of uncertainty is the negative view of competition. German organizations tend to emphasize group decisions, a consultative management style. This is more likely to lead to predictability in behavior. Germany is famous for including an important role for labor unions in management to reduce conflict and strikes.

Certainty

Germans want to know exactly what to expect and what to do.[143] *Sicherheit* (certainty) is a key German value. To be *sicher* (secure or safe) often means to be free of *Angst*. If something is *sicher*, you can rely on it. Other German words commonly used include *gewiss* (certain) and *Gewissheit* (certainty). These words are connected with the German ideal of *Geborgenheit*, being in a place of safety and protection and existential security, with no *Angst*.

Germans often use the term *Heimat* in a similar way. Properly translated, it means "homeland," but it carries important associated emotions. My German aunt Lena referred to her American summer home and escape from New York City as a *Heimat*, a paradise where she could feel *Geborgenheit* and be free of *Angst*. *Heimat* often means the place where Germans grew up as a child, where parents cared for of them, where surroundings were familiar, where they were sure of what they were doing, where they felt safe and protected. Aunt Lena's sister in Germany told her that whenever she visited she could stay in the room where she grew up, her *Heimat*. She would be free of *Angst* there. Perhaps the worst thing that can happen to Germans is to lose their *Heimat*. It would be like losing their soul.[143]

For Germans, Christmas has some of the same qualities as *Heimat*. It is more than a religious holiday. The many familiar aspects are comforting: the snow, the Christmas tree, the candles, and the foods and drinks. Some traditions go back to the sixteenth century. Although many Germans have become increasingly secular, the Advent wreath, the Christmas tree, and other traditional rituals, continue. The Christmas season is a great protection against *Angst*. Insecurities are dissolved by familiar rituals.[16]

The German language has four colloquial words for certainty: *Bescheid*, *bestimmt*, *genau*, and *klar*. These are frequently used in everyday conversations. According to the Duden German dictionary, *Bescheid* comes from the verb *bescheiden* as used in

Amtssprache, the language of officials or bureaucrats, and refers to a decision by authorities. In everyday language it means knowing with certainty what to do in a given situation.

Saying *ganz stimmt* means "quite certainly" or "for sure." *Genau* can mean "precise," but it is often used to answer a question by saying "certainly." *Klar* means "clear" but is also "certainly." Often *Alles klar!* is "now I understand everything what you mean" but also to indicate no more doubts: "now I am certain I know all I need to know." The frequent use of all these words conveying certainty indicates how important it is for Germans to protect against *Angst*.[143]

One antidote to insecurity is activity. Even assertiveness and arrogance can help calm inner insecurity. The oft-noted stiffness of the German demeanor may be a defense against doubts and uncertainties. Germans tend to insist that they know the right thing to do and others should take German ways as a model. Germans may act as if they were schoolmasters and even express some German chauvinism, all in the service of quelling their own insecurities.[16]

Conservatism

Historically, German society has been politically conservative. During the turmoil of the 1920s and early 1930s, Germans had a choice between the Communists and the Nazis who wanted a return to traditional values. Political conservatism resists change and prefers safe, traditional forms of institutions and behavior. The Nazis won over the German people because they promised the same level of security as religion does.[155] Germans saw Hitler as a savior.

Surveys in the Federal Republic of Germany before it combined with Communist East Germany showed nearly 10 percent of the population with extreme right-wing political views.[156] German Americans are also more conservative than the average American. According to the General Social Survey, they tend to vote Republican. In fact, all the American presidents with a German heritage have been Republicans: Hoover, Eisenhower, "Dutch" Reagan, and Donald Trump.

CULTURES

Conservatism can be thought of as a generalized susceptibility to experiencing threat or anxiety in the face of uncertainty. There is evidence it is a heritable personality trait. Researchers have found political conservatism negatively associated with openness to experience and uncertainty tolerance and positively associated with needs for order, structure, and closure as well as fear of threat and loss.[157][158][159]

On the spectrum of stimulus uncertainty, art ranges from simple and representational to abstract. Liberals tend to have the extrovert's need for stimulation, excitement, change, and risk, so they tend to like abstract art. The opposite is true of conservatives. Not surprisingly, during the Nazi era, representational art was popular.[160] Conservatives also seem to prefer familiar music over unfamiliar music.[161]

Low Context Cultures

Anthropologist Edward T. Hall sees German culture as "low context".[162] People in "low context" cultures emphasize information. They want context, explicit details in communications, to create certainty. They are high in uncertainty avoidance. Low context culture requires complexity, duplication, and structure to guarantee full communication.

In Germany, people seek full communication by means of detailed writing and talking. There is little reliance on implicit information. People from "high context" cultures like America can feel that Germans say too much, belaboring the obvious. Americans can say about Germans that there is "too muchness."[163]

High context communications often involve people who for various reasons already have more certainty in their communications. The individuals may know one another and trust that uncertainties and unknowns will not arise, are sure to be worked out, or don't really matter. Much information is transmitted in indirect, non-verbal ways. Simple gestures can be very important. Listeners will pay close attention since important facts may be read "in between the lines."

When the German auto firm Daimler merged with Chrysler in 1998, there was an immediate clash of cultures. At their first joint board meeting with Chrysler, the Germans began with an extensive introductory statement, including the history of the company, its various models, and its future prospects. They provided detailed background information and used lots of transparencies. What Americans termed "a train-wreck of a presentation" lasted almost two hours. The Germans, coming from a low context culture, believed that communications must be very full and explicit.

The Americans from Chrysler presented their firm in a much simpler fashion. They went straight to their models, using showy effects and easy-to-remember statements. Their approach was like that of an enthusiastic salesman—lots of smiles and jokes—and only thirty-five minutes long. Since Germans view business as very serious, they did not appreciate the humor and the lack of attention to details. The Germans thought the Chrysler presentation was superficial and way too optimistic. In contrast, Chrysler's CEO complained to a Stuttgart newspaper that the Germans were armed with tons of overhead transparencies and colored charts that amounted to information overkill.

Explicit information is less necessary for Americans, who often depend on implicit information derived from personal relationships. Germans, with their excessive information, are sometimes seen as intellectually arrogant.

Rules are also important in low context cultures. Without rules, Germans can't feel comfortable with a task, a job description, or work expectations. For Germans, eye contact is also valuable in providing additional explicit context, evidence of listening and respect for the speaker. Often a German will nod and say *"ja"* to indicate he is listening. It is part of the necessary context added to the low context situation typical of German communications.

Expertise

Germans emphasize information to provide security and avoid uncertainty. Eugen Diesel noted a "German passion for imparting information, for instructing others." On the importance of knowledge, Diesel suggested, "Nowhere else in the world is criticism of any professional activity so quickly resented as in Germany, where the man and his calling are one and the same thing.

CULTURES

The specialist and the expert hold sway, and criticism of a man's work is always taken as a personal criticism."[47]

People in Germany often use expertise to provide context for communications, and it is a much bigger part of German culture than American culture. Germans value knowledge and technical ability. Many German managers are trained in engineering. Technical knowledge is respected, and experts are seldom questioned.

A comparison of engineers in Germany and in the U.S. found the Germans were oriented toward a secure professional (specialist or expert) career, while American engineers wanted eventually to move into administrative careers in order to get ahead.[164] A study comparing German and American middle managers similarly showed the Germans emphasizing expertise more than Americans.[165]

If a German leader seems to lack technical ability, he will be scrutinized closely. Adhering to plans and making clear decisions are also important aspects of leadership in Germany. Once a decision is made from the top, subordinates will honor it because those in power are assumed to know best or have the most technical ability.

Because of this emphasis on technical expertise, management courses like those in American business schools did not begin to be offered in Germany until the 1980s. Many Germans believed that if management was a separate discipline it would breed selfishness, disloyalty, bureaucratic maneuvering, short-term thinking, and a dangerous tendency to neglect quality in production. Technical expertise and teamwork were more important.

A reflection of the importance of expertise in Germany is that the ratio of nurses to doctors in hospitals is relatively low compared to the United States.[166, 167] The doctor as expert is more important in Germany.

The German emphasis on experts appears in scholarly work. Germany is famous for Marx, Freud, Weber, and others who promoted all-encompassing theories. Germans had a relative disdain for the specifics of empirical research. In contrast, American social science progresses by gathering data and using statistical tests of significance, a relatively uncertain process compared to postulating grand theories.

Anthropologist Hall emphasized that the "front" presented to others in Germany was very important. Don't admit mistakes, and never show incompetence in anything.[168]

Part of uncertainty avoidance in Germany is the focus on product quality and service. Mercedes-Benz, Porsche, and BMW all emphasize it. German managers describe it as *Leistungswettbewerb*, competition for excellence in products and services. Quality can provide a sense of security, with products and services often advertised as "clean" or "safe" to use. Consumers prefer quality and dependable products that can be used for an extended time. Consumers in countries like the United States, with low uncertainty avoidance, do not depend as much on reliability in their purchasing decisions; they think that if something fails, they will just buy another.

Directness

Germany's low context culture is oriented towards directness and explicitness, not leaving things to chance. If a German asks a coworker how they are, the response will be honest, direct, and full. The coworker is liable to tell about his entire day, leaving no details out, in order not to miss the essence of the truth of the answer. Questioning should also be full, so that no important information is withheld.

In contrast, American high context culture accentuates informality and the personal. Americans often want to be liked and socially accepted. They are influenced by the opinions others have of them. Being outgoing is the way to make friends, even in business. Americans will reveal personal details to others even if they don't know them well. Social acceptance is important; acquaintances are often referred to as "friends," and compliments are given freely and expected in return. Americans might ask: "Do you want to be right, or do you want to be liked?" In his 1835 account of America, Alexis de Tocqueville wrote that in dealing with strangers, Americans seem to be impatient with the slightest criticism and to be insatiable for praise. In contrast, the Germans view compliments as beside the point. Saying "well done" is redundant; it's taken for granted. Americans can grin at a bad situation and suggest making a positive out of a negative. Germans might say that is mathematically impossible.

German business conversations emphasize formality and content instead of personal relationships. Germans want to be perceived as credible and objective. They have fact-oriented, often academic, discussions. The goal is to get at the truth. Germans aren't afraid to explore all sides of an issue, even if it means being unpleasant and confrontational. They are generally very direct, offering criticism. Because the personal element is marginalized, a German subordinate can confront his boss, flatly stating "No, you are wrong!" A heated discussion can follow, with points being made aggressively, sometimes belligerently. Then each can walk away unharmed, their relationship unchanged. An American would be very uncomfortable with such a conversation. German directness can be disconcerting to Americans. Not surprisingly, Americans often see Germans as opinionated and argumentative know-it-alls.

The Germans, for their part, see Americans as superficial and naïve. A German immigrant told me: "Americans are so polite and so general and vague. Americans never say no. Everything has to be positive. I am direct and honest." Americans think her rude, but she grew up that way. "We feel we have a better relationship with people when we are honest. We can trust and rely on each other."

Planning and Rules

Planning is yet another way in which context is supplied in German culture to avoid uncertainty. German planning is extremely thorough, with each aspect of a project examined in great detail. Not surprisingly, when some German researchers went to IBM in the United States, American employees complained that they planned too much. The American approach is to rely more on trial and error and to focus on goals rather than on planning.[169] However, once planning in Germany is done, projects can move very quickly and deadlines are met. Germans do not like surprises. Sudden changes in a business transaction, even if they provide advantages, are disliked.

THE GERMAN MIND

German companies' goals and strategy are generally long-term. Businesses in Germany are focused on planning for the future and on sustaining the company. In America there is more worry about performance over a shorter time period, even quarterly. The German long-term orientation shapes the way that many managers think about the people in work teams and the way tasks are organized.

Still another German coping mechanism to reduce conflict and uncertainty is to set up and adhere to rules. Low context cultures have a lot of rules. Rules allow individuals to avoid making autonomous judgments. Germany has many formal and informal rules. Germans often try to ascertain if there rules they can follow that apply to a situation or part of life.[23] Rules help a low context culture like Germany function efficiently.

Alexis de Tocqueville said that revolutions never took place in Germany because the police forbade them. Vladimir Lenin felt that German revolutionaries would stop to buy tickets before they dared occupy a railroad station. A Communist takeover attempt of Berlin in 1919 was foiled when a guard noted that Berlin authorities had not signed orders for the revolutionary Karl Liebknecht.

Americans, on the other hand, often minimize formal and informal rules and rituals to govern social conduct. Americans sometimes prefer the flexibility that ambiguity offers. Taking risks is often seen as courageous, and trying out new things is encouraged. Though Americans have some general social norms, including some remaining puritanism regarding drinking and sex (e.g., drinking by teens and exposure of breasts in public), they seem more relaxed and friendly, while they think of Germans as "uptight" because they follow so many rules of behavior.

When Germans follow their rules, they perceive order instead of potential conflict and uncertainty. The German love of rules leads to their mania for correction: "Can't you read? Keep to the right! Take your place at the rear!" Germans expect pedestrians to wait if the crossing sign at an intersection says "Don't Walk." If there is no traffic, an American will cross despite the prohibition, perhaps triggering a disapproving look from a waiting German. And many Americans jaywalk, which is illegal in Germany. It is sometimes said that everything is prohibited in Germany unless there is a sign allowing it, for example, "Walking on the grass is permitted."

Hitler was especially popular after he eliminated the lawlessness on the streets common during the Weimar era. Similarly, the United States cracked down on Vietnam War protesters under President Nixon and his German American aides John Ehrlichman and H. R. Haldeman.

Eugen Diesel noted that although Germany is largely an honest country, businesspeople have to be very careful not to fall into a legal trap. If there is a legal stipulation, it will be honored, even if what's permitted is immoral and dishonest.

Rules played an important part in Uber's failure in Germany. Uber achieved tremendous success in the United States by bending rules in true Silicon Valley fashion. Even though some local authorities resisted the unlicensed cab service, the federal government was reluctant to intervene. America also has Airbnb and other start-ups benefiting from the sharing economy. With its billions of venture capital, Uber thought it could go to any other country and simply force its way in, as it did in the United States. But it ignored the fact that German culture places greater importance on firm rules and regulations.

In Germany, governments require ride-sharing firms to institute health exams and security checks and get state-issued licenses, and all these regulations are enforced by local transportation agencies. Germans couldn't turn a blind eye to a company violating the rules. Uber was banned in much of Germany.

Also, since Germans dislike uncertainty, people were not eager to jump on the bandwagon of creative disruption and test radical business models. Take a ride in a unlicensed taxi where the driver is not liable for his actions? Not only radically new, but also possibly dangerous. Uber retrenched and left many Germany cities.

German industries tend to work closely with relevant governmental agencies, adhering to government standards, policies, and regulations. Virtually all German products are subject to norms established through consultation between industry and government, with strong inputs from management associations, chambers of commerce, and trade unions. Everything in Germany, even a screw, seems to have an assigned DIN (*deutsche-industrie-norm*) identification number.

Like rules, Germans prefer routines. An American survey done after the end of the Second World War revealed how lack of a routine can bother Germans. Regular and heavy enemy bombing was less damaging to their morale than moderate but irregular bombing.[170]

Systematization and Rationality

Systematization is another way of dealing with uncertainty. Germans like to see the reasons for every step of what they are doing. They will often take a principle and trace it back to its ultimate origins and forward to its application.[23] A study of adolescents found Germans, more than Americans, agreeing with the statement: "A child should never be asked to do anything unless he is told why he is asked to do it."[39] German meetings are also systematic. However, decisions, once made, are generally final. Those who do not share this systematic style are considered poorly organized.[171]

German rationality is also a reflection of high uncertainty avoidance. Germans try to minimize unknowns and unusual circumstances by proceeding with changes step by step, and by relying on formal procedures rather than being pragmatic. The research that obtained self-descriptions by Germans and Americans found rationality, objectivity, and realism emphasized by Germans and absent in the self-descriptions of Americans.[25]

Projects in Germany are thoroughly researched, providing structure in what may be ambiguous situations. In contrast, Americans often value "common sense."

People in low context countries like Germany seem to prefer deductive thinking as a means of avoiding uncertainty. Germans typically need to understand the philosophies behind a new proposal before they are motivated to take action. They believe in the maxim "think before you act." Their textbooks typically begin with chapters on the philosophy or principles behind the subject matter, quoting experts and philosophers. Then follows a deduction to a theory. The last chapters of a textbook will focus on applications.

In countries like America with its high context culture, textbooks are often pragmatic and full of inductive thinking. Their first chapters will have case studies, samples, and descriptions of what is found in practice. After that, the book will often inductively come up with a "best practice." In such cultures, people are typically action-oriented in their thinking and have slogans like "just do it" and "whatever works." There is less need to fend off the uncertainty of real-life complexity.

Avoiding Uncertainty

In 2011 to 2013, Silicon Valley had thirty-two billion dollars of venture capital available, while in Germany there was only two billion available.[172] German companies, while highly innovative, often remained small because of a lack of financial resources. An example is Mytaxi, started a half a year earlier than Uber, but unable to scale up its business on a global basis. It couldn't raise enough money from venture capital even though its technology worked well and customers liked the product. In contrast, Americans were eager to fund new companies regardless of uncertainties and a high frequency of failures. That's how Uber cornered the world's ride-sharing business.

In America, trying out new things is encouraged. In Germany everything has to be structured and planned carefully, and precedents and tradition are important. This phrase is often used: *Das haben wir schon immer so gemacht*, "We always did it that way." The focus on uncertainty avoidance means that Germany finds it hard to accumulate venture capital.

Germany and the U.S. treat innovation quite differently. Silicon Valley firms usually focus on the core function of a product, then respond to customer feedback. German companies, trying to achieve the perfect product, often spend a much longer time in development and create a product with many different functions and then find out that customers ignore most of the functions. German business owners also fear that their ideas will be stolen. Start-ups in Silicon Valley are more afraid that they will get excluded from the flow of ideas. They believe ideas usually improve when shared.

Germany and Japan, both with very high levels of uncertainty avoidance, have nevertheless become industrial powerhouses. They improve production processes continuously and work towards product perfection. But these days, it seems more important to build disruptive innovations. Germany and Japan may need to modify their fear of uncertainty. Perhaps Germany's million new immigrants will spark more open and flexible mindsets. Immigrants seem more comfortable with uncertainty.

The contrast in low and high context styles became evident when the United States passed the Sarbanes-Oxley Act requiring CEOs and CFOs to swear that their company's financial statements were truthful. Americans were quite ready to sign from the start; they trusted that everything was OK. In Germany, the new law ignited debate in the press and in boardrooms of companies doing business in the United States. Germans said things like, "We can't sign the statement because we didn't do the figures. They were done by the accounting department." There wasn't full information. It was too uncertain.

Monochronic Culture

Another distinctive aspect of German culture is time management. According to anthropologist Hall, there are two different orientations to time. In monochronic cultures, time is linear and sequential and only one thing at a time is focused on. This is related to a preference for truth and directness.

In polychronic cultures, many things involving many people can occur simultaneously. This orientation is most common in Mediterranean and Latin cultures including France, Italy, Greece, and Mexico, as well as some Eastern and African cultures. America, with its ethnic diversity, sometimes leans in this direction. The trains are not always on time, and people are not too bothered by such uncertainty.

People from polychronic cultures start and end meetings at flexible times and take breaks when it seems appropriate. They don't take lateness personally, are comfortable with a high flow of information, sometimes overlap in talking, and are even attuned to unspoken thoughts.

In contrast, people from monochronic cultures prefer a strict time schedule for meetings and breaks and stick to an agenda, rely on specific, detailed, and explicit communication, prefer to talk in sequence, and view lateness as disrespectful.

In Germany, people who show up exactly on time make others feel more certain and more trusting of the person. Adherence to schedules and the timing of tasks throughout the workday is important. The trains run more nearly on time. Germans also like to be precise about timing. Rather than saying "in about a month," they might say "in thirty days." Being on time can sometimes be an obsession. Instead of risking an arrival a minute late due to traffic, a German might play it safe and plan to arrive a half hour early.

Germans value precision in whatever they do. It's part of the language itself. German sentences are often sprinkled with adverbs, adjectives, and conjunctions that combine the abstract and the concrete. The French might say "fresh bread," the German, "freshly baked bread."[16] Lipstick advertisements might give the temperature below which the lipstick would begin to cake. Once, a small whale from the North Sea got trapped in the Main River. Radio and newspapers noted the precise location of every sighting and how many times per minute the animal exhaled.[173]

Germans sometimes fear to omit the smallest details. It is said that Germany has more traffic signs than any other country, warning about all possible dangers. They can overlook the scenery while attending to all the warning signs.[16]

Compartmentalization

Another important part of monochronic cultures is compartmentalization, separating activities and units so that there is no overlap. This simplifies matters, reducing uncertainty.

In Germany, different business units such as finance, engineering, sales, and human resources typically will have their own spaces. There is also task compartmentalization, with the working environment more structured and layered. Part of a monochronic culture like Germany is a tendency to isolate and divide many aspects of individual lives into discrete, independent units.[174]

THE GERMAN MIND

A study of German research chemists found they preferred to work almost exclusively in the office, rarely in the laboratory. Germans also had a tendency to keep to themselves. In contrast, in the United States professional chemists liked to do some of their laboratory work themselves, even if they had lab technicians that could do that it for them.[175]

Silicon Valley emphasizes the free exchange of ideas and a disregard for hierarchy. Even a student with a good idea may get access to people with capital and know-how. People love to meet others in cafes or at parties, and to share their ideas. In Germany, these things are less likely.

Low context and monochrome cultures with their compartmentalization, systematization, planning, reliability, rules, and expertise seek to avoid uncertainty and anxiety. That's important for German organizations and individuals. These cultural structures seem compatible with conscientiousness and foster the industriousness and economic prowess characteristic of Germany.

Germans and Americans

Studies of joint projects between Germans and Americans reveal some of their cultural and personality differences. A researcher found that at the very beginning of such a joint project the Germans showed a greater need for detailed information and discussion.[176] The Germans tended to see the process from an engineering point of view, considering all of the difficulties that might arise then planning hypothetical solutions. They wanted to make sure everything would be done correctly and that every possible element would be kept under control. The Germans also expected that all team members would share knowledge at the beginning by sketching out their previous experiences. It was essential to reach a consensus so as to rapidly implement a strategy. The researcher concluded that German decision-making concentrated on identifying problems, their history, and their components, with less discussion about results.

In contrast, the action-oriented Americans found these discussions annoying and boring. The exchange of so much information seemed a waste of time, "paralysis through analysis."

CULTURES

No matter how good a plan was, American thinking went, it would be modified along the way. The Americans hoped to speed up the process and get down to work. In American thinking, the problem solving should start out with a short brainstorming session to define goals and a series of approximate milestones. Creativity should be the watchword. In addition, the Americans wanted to keep all options open, perceiving any project as a trial-and-error process. Decision-making was more open-ended, concentrating on a mission or a vision.

The Germans felt the Americans were acting without fully understanding the problem. There was too much shooting first and asking questions later. In contrast, the Americans felt the German obsession with making and sticking to plans meant being locked into a rigid formula, with no flexibility during the implementation phase.

Once a plan was established, German team members were able to work relatively independently. In contrast, the Americans typically expected further group meetings and informal communication throughout. The Germans complained that the Americans discussed issues that had already been decided.

Additional problems appeared when Americans were given tasks for which they had not been thoroughly trained. Americans interchanged jobs and learned by doing. Germans were generally better trained and even engineers and executives had been exposed to a mix of the practical and the theoretical. In addition, Germans usually knew the strict rules for doing business in Europe. Whether it was cars or cosmetics or cold cuts, there were norms, guidelines, and documentation that one actually had to study and know.

Germans also assumed decisions made at group meetings were binding. Americans saw them only as guidelines that could be changed if needed. They expected better solutions to evolve.

Leadership can be a major problem in joint projects. A German leader is typically both an expert and a mediator (expected to convince, not order) who tends to vote with the group. During the implementation phase, there was little need for interaction with group members. In contrast, American leaders typically defined goals, made decisions, distributed tasks, and made sure they were done. Motivation and coaching were part of the chain-of-command style. American communication was intense by European standards and continued all the way through to completion and afterwards when out for the celebratory drinks.

This brings up the American emphasis on friendliness. In fact, Americans don't act all that differently at work than they do when they're out bowling with the project team. Germans try to maintain a "work only" relationship with colleagues. They keep work separate from the rest of life. The German desk rarely has family pictures. They also don't invite relative strangers home for supper. There is a German saying, *Dienst ist Dienst und Schnapps ist Schnapps* (work is work and drinking is drinking). For Americans, there is greater interpenetration of work and family life. Americans are also a lot more open to coming into the office on Sunday.

Another observational study of American and German team meetings confirmed some of these findings, including the German emphasis on problem analysis and the American emphasis on solutions. American teams members were also friendlier to one another. In contrast, the Germans did more complaining, seeking someone to blame, or trying to end the discussion early.[177] Another study showed that Germans averaged fifty-two complaining statements in team meetings but only two positive action-planning statements.[178] This could also be due to the German belief in honesty even if it hurts.

9: WARS

Germany's wars have been a major part of its history and have shaped their culture of uncertainty avoidance and *Angst*. Civilians as well as the military have been influenced as far back as the Thirty Years' War (1618-1648), when Catholic and Protestant armies from all over Europe converged to fight in Germany. They killed and raped peasants and seized and destroyed property. The German population dropped from 16 million to 10 million. Even today, Germans speak of the impact of that devastating war.

Militarism

In the eighteenth century Germans still lived in 1,800 independent states that could be in conflict. As Prussia gained power, Frederick the Great decreed that "all inhabitants of the state are born to bear arms." Military drills and strict disciple were enforced by corporal punishment. During much of Frederick's rule, Prussia was in a constant state of war, and men from minor German principalities were forced into his army.

At the beginning of the nineteenth century, Napoleon invaded the German states and forced conquered Germans into his army to invade Russia. Very few came back from that disastrous campaign. Prussia stepped up military training to defeat Napoleon. According to an 1814 Prussian law, recruits of age twenty were required to serve three years in the military, followed by two more years in the reserves and service in the militia for much of the rest of their lives. With its increasing power, Prussia attacked and defeated Denmark and Austria and some of the smaller German states.

After victory in the Franco-Prussian War in 1870, Prussia unified the German states. To prepare for conflict with France or Russia, German military discipline became increasingly severe. Those who didn't obey could be summarily dismissed from the army and lose their pension. A culture of blame and secrecy pervaded officers and enlisted men, with bullying and beatings to enforce sanctions for rule violations.

In the First World War, 13 million Germans were mobilized, two million died and more than four million were wounded. Millions of others suffered from "shell shock"—what today we would term PTSD, post-traumatic stress disorder, with symptoms of anxiety and panic.

In December 1918 the German Board of Public Health reported that 763,000 German civilians had died from starvation and disease due to the Allied naval blockade. The Allies restricted food shipments until six months after the war's end, and an estimated 100,000 more Germans died from starvation.

During Second World War, an estimated 25,000 death sentences were issued by German military court, with about 12,000 carried out. (In the U.S. Army only one man was executed during the war.)[60] Many German civilians were traumatized by Allied carpet bombing of cities. A 1942 British study showed that each ton of incendiary bombs destroyed 13,000 square kilometers of cities. The incendiary bombs used phosphorous, burning victims alive. More than half a million German civilians died from Allied bombing, and fifteen million survivors fled the cities for rural villages. Many children were traumatized by seeing their homes destroyed and family members killed.

As the Red Army reached Germany, up to two million women were raped, sometimes repeatedly. Rapes continued until the winter of 1947-48, when Soviet occupation authorities finally confined troops to strictly guarded posts and camps.[179, 180] In 1945 Hannelore Kohl, later the wife of Chancellor Helmut Kohl, was gang-raped at age twelve along with her mother by Soviet soldiers. She eventually committed suicide.[181] (Rapes by U.S. servicemen numbered 11,000.[182] No comprehensive figures have appeared for British rapes.) French Moroccan troops matched the behavior of Soviet troops in traumatizing German women.[179] Most German families were affected by the war: over four million Germans in the military were killed and over five million wounded.[183]

Estimated civilian deaths from the forced expulsion of ethnic Germans from traditional settlements in Eastern Europe range from 500,000 to over two million. Fleeing women were often subjected to rapes. Hundreds of thousands of small children were part of a forced march to escape the Red Army. The winter of

1944-45 was the coldest in years, and corpses littered the roadsides. Some children were separated from their families, and others saw their mothers and sisters raped. Many children who made it to the West went from camp to camp and thousands died of starvation or froze to death. Orphans and others separated from their families roamed through Germany without shoes or warm clothes. If they did have a bed, many spent most of their time there. Without shoes or warm clothing, they were unable to go to school.[60]

Surviving Germans called the end of the war *Stunde Null* (Time Zero).[184] The country was almost completely devastated. Because the coal mines were destroyed and there were no miners, fuel for winter was in short supply, The census of 1946 counted 36 million females and only 28 million males with most being elderly, invalids, or children.[185] Germans gathered branches or pine cones in the woods to use in place of coal.

Food was very scarce. The Soviets agreed at the Potsdam meetings of August 1945 to ship food from the agricultural territories they occupied in exchange for industrial equipment and products from the British and American zones of occupation—but the Soviets reneged on that deal.

Millions of ethnic Germans who had been expelled from Eastern European enclaves and from the parts of Germany lost to annexation by Poland and Russia flooded into the Western occupied zones, along with many non-German refugees who had fled the communists. Allied occupation forces had to feed them all. Two years after the end of the war, people in West Germany were still on near-starvation diets of 1,040 calories a day (American soldiers averaged 4,200).[186]

Shelter was also scarce. Most West German cities were more than half destroyed. Twenty million people were homeless. Many lived in cellars underneath burnt-out buildings. In the heavily bombed northwestern part of Germany occupied by the British, the average dwelling space for an entire family was nine by six feet. When I first visited Germany fifteen years after war's end, sections of some downtowns of cities were still walled off and in ruins.

Clearly, the Second World War created much suffering for the German people. Of course, by the end of the war and afterward, the earlier disappearance of German Jews into the Holocaust camps had been forgotten even if it had been noted at the time. Only a few "privileged Jews," spouses of Gentiles, remained to be mostly ignored.

Epigenetics and Conscientiousness

Recent research suggests that the effects of trauma may be passed on to subsequent generations by epigenetics. Through a process of methylation, genes can be disrupted or silenced. Some selective marking of DNA can cross generations via gametes. These alternations in phenotype may continue for two or more generations.[187]

The first study of such epigenetic inheritance involved the Dutch experience at the close of the Second World War. Their children later suffered from a variety of maladies as a result of the experiences of their parents' generation.[188, 189] Similar epigenetic inheritance has been found after famine in Sweden.[190] Transgenerational epigenetic influences have been demonstrated for survivors of the Holocaust, the Tutsi genocide, and other victims of mass trauma.[191, 192]

Epigenetic changes can be advantageous when certain events reoccur yet unpredictably. If individuals can foresee the imminence of an environmental threat so defenses can be mounted once the threat materializes, epigenetic changes would be adaptive. Epigenetic modifications such as inhibited behavior seem to be a function of amygdala responsiveness. Research has demonstrated that adults identified as inhibited as toddlers show less arousal of the amygdala in response to novelty than peers who were uninhibited at that early age. Epigenetic methylation and silencing of genes, thereby increasing caution, could well operate to give advantages in facing environmental threats such as famine and conquest.[193]

Traits of conscientiousness—including being frugal, orderly, organized, thorough, and hard-working—could thus be adaptive responses to trauma suffered by earlier generations. So might impulse control, which includes being cautious, self-controlled, and serious.[194] Implementing normative tightness, with strongly enforced rules and low tolerance for deviance, could also be helpful.[195]

It is quite possible that the many German victims of trauma have transmitted their conscientiousness and resultant cultural constraint to later generations, with a possible positive effect on the nation's industriousness.

10: TERROR MANAGEMENT AND NORMS

Germans' marked pessimism about the future despite ongoing prosperity could be due to epigenetics and the history of famine and war traumas. Also pertinent is an American theory of "terror management," or how people deal with thoughts about death. This is not to say that Germans think more about death than other peoples, although the wars could indeed remind some that death eventually awaits all. However, for most people, thoughts about mortality are submerged into the unconscious.

Self-esteem is an important bulwark against feelings of vulnerability and anxiety. Culture plays an important role by providing concepts of reality, standards, and a sense of belonging to something that can endure beyond death.[196, 197]

The process of dealing with anxiety begins early, during the time when the infant needs closeness and positive affection. Infants can develop anxiety and insecurity from the implicit possibility of losing such comforting when the parent is no longer present. At least one study has shown that infants in Germany received less comforting than infants in America, perhaps because mothers were heeding cultural norms encouraging independence by children.[99]

As a child develops, its feelings of comfort become increasingly dependent on meeting specific parental standards. In this way, the child is socialized but often without intellectually and emotionally understanding why particular behaviors are considered good. The child learns what to do and what not to do in order to avoid anxiety. Children come to equate being good with being safe and misbehaving with anxiety and insecurity. As the child's ego develops, defense mechanisms such as denial, projection, isolation, and repression develop to prevent awareness of anxieties.

This parent-pleasing behavior transfers eventually to meeting the expectations of others to remain in good standing in the culture. A person comes to want to do what the culture requires and comes to expect that others will follow those rules and norms, too. Socially determined standards of value are associated with feelings of safety and security. This learning is reinforced when others confirm the rightness of appropriate behavior. Living up to societal standards brings self-esteem, security, and safety. Research shows that high self-esteem will reduce anxiety and anxiety-related defensive behaviors.[198, 199]

With the eventual awareness of mortality, people know parents will die and can't keep providing safety and security forever.[200] People will develop defense mechanisms against everyday anxieties, but A*ngst* over being mortal is harder to defend against. A symbolic sense of immortality can come from believing that culture will outlast one. This sense of belonging can counter the unconscious *Angst* of mortality. This is terror management.

Social Norms

Norms are a community's characteristic patterns of thought and behavior that emanate from their shared social context. What others do and believe is a powerful influence on behavior. Humans are social animals. Self-esteem can depend on fulfilling society's norms and priorities rather than fulfilling personal values.[201] Researchers have shown that self-esteem from adherence to prescriptive cultural norms is often greater than self-esteem from following personal values.[202]

This explains why people often react so negatively to foreigners who possess different sets of normative beliefs. They call into question the home culture's aura of immortality and its ability to buffer anxiety. Contact with other cultures can highlight the arbitrariness of cultural norms, making people feel the beliefs they live by are threatened. This is the source of ethnocentrism and prejudice.[203]

Researchers have validated terror management theory. Subjects with the anxiety-buffering effects of self-esteem display fewer symptoms of physiological arousal.[198] High levels of self-esteem can reduce anxiety and anxiety-related defensive behavior.[198, 199] When individuals find mortality threatened, they strive to enhance self-esteem.[204] As a result, they identify with preferred groups.[205] Following societal norms gives the sense of being a valuable contributor to a meaningful, immortal reality.[206] Longitudinal research has also demonstrated that low self-esteem will eventually foster subsequent anxiety.[207]

Terror management theory also suggests that reminding people of their own mortality can increase their support for a leader. An experiment in the United States that triggered thoughts about the 9/11 attacks showed increased support for President George W. Bush. Did all the fighting and killing in Germany during the Weimar Republic enhance support for Hitler as a prospective "savior" and provider of symbolic immortality?

Research has determined the relevant cultural norms in Germany that might bring comfort and even a sense of immortality. A national survey asked respondents to indicate the general qualities of the German people. The responses were: diligent, ambitious, intelligent, thorough, clean, thrifty, careful, exact, detailed.[208] Many of these qualities fall under conscientiousness, the Big Five syndrome explaining high achievement and high performance.

In a survey reported in the Frankfurter *Allgemeine Zeitung* newspaper in January 2015, respondents were asked: "What are the best characteristics of the Germans?" Of respondents, 79 percent said "diligent" or "industrious"; 76 percent said "punctual"; 71 percent, "orderly"; 66 percent, "reliable" or "certain"; 57 percent, "clean" or "neat"; 56 percent "inventive"; 55 percent "exacting." These "best" characteristics are clearly prescriptive norms or "oughts" indicating social standards that people should follow. The responses indicate the importance of conscientiousness norms for Germans.[209-211] Such norms are crucial for German economic achievement.

A study of thirty-three different cultures showed that norms in Germany are relatively "tight," rather than "loose," with relatively little flexibility allowed in their observance. Germans expect conformity to norms. These conscientiousness norms are rarely optional for Germans. Other societies with looser norms allow more freedom to disobey.[212, 213] And other "tight" cultures may possess norms not associated with high productivity. In Pakistan, for example, there is strictness, but it is in relation to religious norms, not conscientiousness norms that foster industriousness, as in Germany.

Terror management theory, with its linkage of self-esteem to German norms that are essentially conscientiousness norms, provides one more avenue in which German society is able to foster industriousness and economic prowess.

11: PERSONALITY VS. CULTURE

Which is more important, personality or cultural norms? Do existing personalities foster a compatible culture, or does culture develop appropriate personalities? Which most contributes to fostering German economic achievement?

Studies of identical twins have established that conscientiousness and neuroticism are heritable traits. Such personality syndromes are relatively stable over time, also suggesting that they may be primary, rather than culture.[214-216]

Research shows that countries with neurotic personalities have a culture of uncertainty avoidance.[214, 217] People with high neuroticism are tense and have difficult interpersonal interactions. To avoid instability and conflict, organizations adopt rigid rules. Institutions will typify a high uncertainty avoidance and low context culture, with planning, rules, perfectionism, and systemization. However, this is just a relationship with no evidence of causal priority for personality or culture.

Recent research sheds light on which might come first, personalities or cultures. Researchers have compared the typical personalities of West Germans with those in East Germany after the Soviets had occupied and controlled that country for forty-five years. The Communist regimes controlled the economy, education, mass media, and legal institutions, but they didn't change East German personalities. This suggests that personality rather than culture is causally primary.[218]

CONCLUSIONS

What is the main trigger for Germany's prodigious industrial achievements? There is certainly considerable evidence that conscientious personalities are important.

Research also reveals that neurotic personalities are correlated with cultures of uncertainty avoidance. In coping with social interactions, people can emphasize rules, planning, systematization, reliability, and the like to relieve anxieties. Terror management theory also explains how anxiety can be productive—fostering adherence to societal norms, which, in Germany, emphasize conscientiousness and resultant industriousness.

Germany's history of wars also may play a role. Uncertainty avoidance culture helps people cope with the anxieties that are part of war. A low context culture is compatible with that history, including rules, planning, systematization, etc., to foster greater security and greater certainty. This is probably also true of a monochronic approach to time. These aspects of culture can support German personalities that emphasize conscientiousness.

Finally, epigenetic theory suggests that constraint, caution, frugality, and other aspects of conscientiousness may have been a consequence of the warfare and famine often suffered by Germans, an influence that can persist for several generations.

All these forces seem intertwined. A host of psychological and cultural variables seem to explain Germany's economic productivity. However, conscientious personalities seem to be the most important factor. Because conscientiousness has a heritable component, it is likely to persist, and therefore Germany's economic prowess will continue in the foreseeable future.

REFERENCES

1. Staël, O.W. Wight, and F.M. Müller, Germany. 1859, Houghton, Mifflin and company,: Boston, New York.
2. Favazza, A., A critical review of studies of national character. Journal of Operational Psychiatry, 1974. **6**(1): p. 3-30.
3. Helmreich, W.B., The things they say behind your back: Stereotypes and the myths behind them. 1982: Transaction Publishers.
4. Karlins, M., T.L. Coffman, and G. Walters, On the fading of social stereotypes: Studies in three generations of college students. Journal of Personality and Social Psychology, 1969. **13**(1): p. 1.
5. Farver, J.A.M., et al., Toy stories aggression in children's narratives in the United States, Sweden, Germany, and Indonesia. Journal of Cross-Cultural Psychology, 1997. **28**(4): p. 393-420.
6. McGranahan, D.V. and M. Janowitz, Studies of German youth. The Journal of Abnormal and Social Psychology, 1946. **41**(1): p. 3.
7. Schaffner, B., Father land: a study of authoritarianism in the German family. 1948: Columbia University Press.
8. Zimbardo, P.G., C. Maslach, and C. Haney, Reflections on the Stanford prison experiment: Genesis, transformations, consequences. Obedience to authority: Current perspectives on the Milgram paradigm, 2000: p. 193-237.
9. Lederer, G., Authoritarianism in German adolescents: Trends and cross-cultural comparisons, in strength and weakness. 1993, Springer. p. 182-198.
10. Oppenheim, A., J. Torney, and R. Farnen, Civic education in ten countries. 1975, New York, Wiley.
11. Almond, G.A. and S. Verba, The civic culture revisited: An analytic study. 1980.
12. König, R., Family and authority: The German father in 1955. The Sociological Review, 1957. **5**(1): p. 107-127.
13. Mitscherlich, A., E. Mosbacher, and F.K. Ringer, Society without the Father. 1972.
14. Hellpach, W.H., *Der deutsche Charakter.-Bonn: Athenäum-Verl. 1954. 245 S. 8*. 1954: Athenäum-Verlag.

15. Noelle-Neumann, E. and B. Strümpel, *Macht Arbeit krank. Macht Arbeit glücklich*, 1984. **2**.
16. Nuss, B., *Das Faust-Syndrom: ein Versuch über die Mentalität der Deutschen*. 1993: Bouvier.
17. Reynolds, B.K., A cross-cultural study of values of Germans and Americans. International Journal of Intercultural Relations, 1984. **8**(3): p. 269-278.
18. Crott, H.W. and P.B. Baltes, Desirability of personality dimensions: Auto-and heteroperceptions by American and German college students. The Journal of Social Psychology, 1973. **91**(1): p. 15-27.
19. Ray, J.J. and W. Kiefl, Authoritarianism and achievement motivation in contemporary West Germany. The Journal of Social Psychology, 1984. **122**(1): p. 3-19.
20. Moore, S., The Fourth Reich? The EU-an emerging German empire. 2016, Great Britiain: Jollies Publishing. 352.
21. Wilterdink, N., Images of national character. Society, 1994. **32**(1): p. 43-51.
22. Costa, P.T. and R.R. McCrae, Four ways five factors are basic. Personality and Individual Differences, 1992. **13**(6): p. 653-665.
23. Peabody, D., National characteristics. 1985, Cambridge [Cambridgeshire]; New York: Cambridge University Press ix, 256 p.
24. Digman, J.M., Personality structure: Emergence of the five-factor model. Annual review of psychology, 1990. **41**(1): p. 417-440.
25. Greene, J.B., A phenomenological analysis of self-descriptive essays written by West German and American students. 1988, California School of Professional Psychology: Berkeley. p. 330.
26. Savelsberg, J.J., Religion, historical contingencies, and institutional conditions of criminal punishment: The German case and beyond. Law & Social Inquiry, 2004. **29**(2): p. 373-401.
27. Rammsayer, T., P. Netter, and W.H. Vogel, A neurochemical model underlying differences in reaction times between introverts and extraverts. Personality and Individual Differences, 1993. **14**(5): p. 701-712.
28. Golde, G., Catholics and Protestants: agricultural modernization in two German villages. 1975, New York: Academic Press.

REFERENCES

29. Basabe, N. and M. Ros, Cultural dimensions and social behavior correlates: individualism-collectivism and power distance. International Review of Social Psychology, 2005. **18**(1): p. 189-225.
30. Boddy, J., A. Carver, and K. Rowley, Effects of positive and negative verbal reinforcement on performance as a function of extraversion-introversion: Some tests of Gray's theory. Personality and Individual Differences, 1986. **7**(1): p. 81-88.
31. Lynn, R., National differences in anxiety and extroversion. Normal Personality Processes: Progress in Experimental Personality Research, 2014. **11**: p. 213.
32. Lewin, K., Some social-psychological differences between the United States and Germany. Journal of Personality, 1936. **4**(4): p. 265-293.
33. Burger, J.M., J.A. Oakman, and N.G. Bullard, Desire for control and the perception of crowding. Personality and Social Psychology Bulletin, 1983. **9**(3): p. 475-479.
34. Hall, E.T., The hidden dimension. 1966.
35. Hall, E.T. and M.R. Hall, Understanding cultural differences. 1989: Intercultural press.
36. McGoldrick, M., J. Giordano, and N. Garcia-Preto, Ethnicity & family therapy. 3rd ed. 2005, New York: Guilford. 796 p.
37. Browning, E., Side by side: Computer chip project brings rivals together, but the cultures clash; Foreign work habits get in the way of creative leaps, hobbling joint research. Softball is not the answer. The Wall Street Journal, 1994: p. A1.
38. Scherer, K.R., H.G. Wallbott, and A.B. Summerfield, Experiencing emotion: A cross-cultural study. 1986: Cambridge University Press.
39. McClelland, D.C., et al., Obligations to self and society in the United States and Germany. The Journal of Abnormal and Social Psychology, 1958. **56**(2): p. 245.
40. Küsell, H.-R., Personality profiles of young adults in the United States and Germany: childhood antecedents and cross-generational change and stabilty, in Political and Social Science. 1993, New School for Social Research: New York, New York. p. 228.
41. Winawer, H. and N. Wetzel, German families. Ethnicity and family therapy, 1996: p. 496-516.

42. Hareli, S., K. Kafetsios, and U. Hess, A cross-cultural study on emotion expression and the learning of social norms. Frontiers in Psychology, 2015. **6**.
43. Loevinger, J., The meaning and measurement of ego development. American Psychologist, 1966. **21**(3): p. 195.
44. Loevinger, J., Measuring ego development. 2014: Psychology Press.
45. Thoresen, C.J., et al., The big five personality traits and individual job performance growth trajectories in maintenance and transitional job stages. Journal of Applied Psychology, 2004. **89**(5): p. 835.
46. Barrick, M.R. and M.K. Mount, The big five personality dimensions and job performance: a meta-analysis. Personnel Psychology, 1991. **44**(1): p. 1-26.
47. Diesel, E. and W.D. Robson-Scott, Germany and the Germans. 1931, New York,: The Macmillan company. ix, 306 p.
48. Gross, J., *Die Deutschen*. 1969: Scheffler.
49. Brodbeck, F.C., M. Frese, and M. Javidan, Leadership made in Germany: Low on compassion, high on performance. The Academy of Management Executive, 2002. **16**(1): p. 16-29.
50. Bales, R.F. and T. Parsons, Family, socialization and interaction process. 2014: Routledge.
51. Lewis, R.D., When cultures collide: leading accross cultures. Boston: Nicholas Brealey, 2006.
52. Hayman, R., Brecht: A biography. 1983, Oxford University Press: New York. p. 423.
53. Rose, N. *https://mappalicious.com/2015/01/07/theres-a-lack-of-positive-words-in-the-german-language/*. [cited 2017 August 18].
54. Trautmann, G., *Die hässlichen Deutschen?: Deutschland im Spiegel der westlichen und östlichen Nachbarn*. 1991: Wissenschaftliche Buchgesellschaft.
55. Forgas, J.P., An unobtrusive study of reactions to national stereotypes in four European countries. The Journal of Social Psychology, 1976. **99**(1): p. 37-42.
56. Heuss, T., German character and history. 1957.
57. Bailey, G., Germans: the biography of an obsession. 1991: Free Press.
58. Dundes, A., Life is like a chicken coop ladder : a portrait of German culture through folklore. 1984, New York: Columbia University Press. xi, 174 p.

REFERENCES

59. Rodnick, D., Postwar Germans: an anthropologist's account. 1948: Yale University Press.
60. Ende, A., Battering and neglect: Children in Germany, 1860-1978. The Journal of Psychohistory, 1979. **7**(3): p. 249.
61. Shabecoff, A., Bringing up Hans und Gretel, in *New York Times*. 1966.
62. Nurge, E., Blue light in the village: daily life in a German village in 1965-66. 1977, Lincoln: University of Nebraska Press.
63. Diesel, E., Germany and the Germans. 1931.
64. Schaffner, B.H., Fatherland; a study of authoritarianism in the German family. 1948, New York,: Columbia Univ. Press. xii, 203 p.
65. Murtha, T.C., R. Kanfer, and P.L. Ackerman, Toward an interactionist taxonomy of personality and situations: An integrative situational—dispositional representation of personality traits. Journal of Personality and Social Psychology, 1996. **71**(1): p. 193.
66. Greeley, A. and W. McCready, Ethnicity in the US. 1974, New York: John Wiley.
67. Wieland, G.F., Stubborn & liking it: Einstein & other Germans in America. 2016, Ann Arbor, Michigan: George F. Wieland. 312 p.
68. Mintzberg, H., A note on that dirty word "Efficiency". Interfaces, 1982. **12**(5): p. 101-105.
69. Levine, R.V. and A. Norenzayan, The pace of life in 31 countries. Journal of Cross-Cultural Psychology, 1999. **30**(2): p. 178-205.
70. Roberts, B.W.O.C., S Stark, The structure of conscientiousness: An empirical investigation based on seven major personality questionnaires. Personnel Psychology, 2005. **58**: p. 103-139.
71. Judge, T.A., et al., Personality and leadership: a qualitative and quantitative review. Journal of Applied Psychology, 2002. **87**(4): p. 765.
72. Judge, T.A., et al., The big five personality traits, general mental ability, and career success across the life span. Personnel Psychology, 1999. **52**(3): p. 621-652.
73. Salgado, J.F., The Five Factor Model of personality and job performance in the European Community. 1997, American Psychological Association.

74. Fallon, J.D., et al., Conscientiousness as a predictor of productive and counterproductive behaviors. Journal of Business and Psychology, 2000. **15**(2): p. 339-349.
75. Ones, D.S., C. Viswesvaran, and A.D. Reiss, Role of social desirability in personality testing for personnel selection: The red herring. 1996, American Psychological Association.
76. Hough, L.M. and F.L. Oswald, Personality testing and industrial–organizational psychology: Reflections, progress, and prospects. Industrial and Organizational Psychology, 2008. **1**(3): p. 272-290.
77. Schmidt, F.L. and J.E. Hunter, The validity and utility of selection methods in personnel psychology: Practical and theoretical implications of 85 years of research findings. Psychological Bulletin, 1998. **124**(2): p. 262.
78. Hurtz, G.M. and J.J. Donovan, Personality and job performance: The Big Five revisited. Journal of Applied Psychology, 2000. **85**(6): p. 869-879.
79. Cubel, M., et al., Do personality traits affect productivity? Evidence from the laboratory. The Economic Journal, 2016. **126**(592): p. 654-681.
80. O'Flaherty, J.C., Inwardness - The key to German institutions. American-German Review, 1955. **21**(3): p. 30-33.
81. Martindale, D., Community, character, and civilization. 1963, Glencoe, IL: Free Press. 467.
82. Dahrendorf, R., Society and democracy in Germany. 1st ed. 1967, Garden City, N.Y.,: Doubleday. xvi, 482 p.
83. Dumont, L., German ideology: From France to Germany and back. 1994: University of Chicago Press.
84. Moore, M., A cross-cultural comparison of value systems. European Journal of Social Psychology, 1976.
85. O'Flaherty, J.C., Inwardness - The key to German institutions (Part II). American-German Review, 1955. **21**(4): p. 23-26.
86. Laqueur, W., Germany today: a personal report. 1985: Weidenfeld & Nicolson.
87. Nuss, Bernard, *Das Faust-Syndrom: Ein Versuch über die Mentalität der Deutschen*. 1993, Bonn: Bouvier. 213 p.
88. Schütt, P. and E.B. Cowling, *Waldsterben*, a general decline of forests in central Europe: symptoms, development and possible causes. Plant Disease, 1985. **69**(7): p. 548-558.

REFERENCES

89. Skelly, J.M. and J.L. Innes, *Waldsterben* in the forests of central Europe and eastern North America: Fantasy or reality? Plant Disease, 1994. **78**(11): p. 1021-1032.
90. Riesman, D., et al., The lonely crowd: a study of the changing American character. Abridged and rev. ed. 2001, New Haven ; London: Yale Nota Bene. lxxii, 315 p.
91. Simmons, C.H., A.V. Kolke, and H. Shimizu, Attitudes toward romantic love among American, German, and Japanese students. The Journal of Social Psychology, 1986. **126**(3): p. 327-336.
92. Adolph, D., S. Schneider, and J. Margraf, German anxiety barometer—clinical and everyday-life anxieties in the general population. Frontiers in Psychology, 2016. **7**.
93. Gray, J.A. and N. McNaughton, The neuropsychology of anxiety. 2000, Oxford University Press.
94. Bijttebier, P., et al., Gray's Reinforcement Sensitivity Theory as a framework for research on personality–psychopathology associations. Clinical Psychology Review, 2009. **29**(5): p. 421-430.
95. Carver, C.S., Two distinct bases of inhibition of behaviour: viewing biological phenomena through the lens of psychological theory. European Journal of Personality, 2008. **22**: p. 388-390.
96. Spence, J.T. and K.W. Spence, The motivational components of manifest anxiety: Drive and drive stimuli. Anxiety and behavior, 1966: p. 291-326.
97. Ainsworth, M., et al., Patterns of attachment. 1978, Hillsdale, NJ: Erlbaum.
98. Grossmann, K.E., et al., German children's behavior towards their mothers at 12 months and their fathers at 18 months in Ainsworth's Strange Situation. International Journal of Behavioral Development, 1981. **4**(2): p. 157-181.
99. Grossmann, K., et al., Maternal sensitivity and newborns' orientation responses as related to quality of attachment in northern Germany. Monographs of the Society for Research in Child Development, 1985: p. 233-256.
100. Grossmann, K., K.E. Grossmann, and H. Kindler, Early care and the roots of attachment and partnership representations. Attachment from infancy to adulthood. The major longitudinal studies, 2005: p. 98-136.
101. Zimmermann, P., et al., Attachment and adolescents' emotion regulation during a joint problem-solving task with

a friend. International Journal of Behavioral Development, 2001. **25**(4): p. 331-343.
102. Main, M., E. Hesse, and N. Kaplan, Predictability of attachment behavior and representational processes at 1, 6, and 19 years of age. Attachment from infancy to adulthood: The major longitudinal studies, 2005: p. 245-304.
103. Barzini, L., The Europeans. 1983: Penguin Books.
104. Schein, E.H., Kurt Lewin's change theory in the field and in the classroom: Notes toward a model of managed learning. Systems Practice, 1996. **9**(1): p. 27-47.
105. Strauman, T.J. and E.T. Higgins, Automatic activation of self-discrepancies and emotional syndromes: when cognitive structures influence affect. Journal of Personality and Social Psychology, 1987. **53**(6): p. 1004.
106. Metraux, R., The consequences of wrongdoing: An analysis of story completions by German children. Childhood in contemporary cultures. Margaret Mead and Martha Wolfenstein, eds, 1955: p. 306-323.
107. Bellak, L. and M. Antell, An intercultural study of aggressive behavior on children's playgrounds. American Journal of Orthopsychiatry, 1974. **44**(4): p. 503.
108. Online, S. *Umfrage in Deutschland: Fast die Hälfte der Eltern Schlägt ihre Kinder.* 2012 [cited 2016 June 20, 2016]; Available from: http://www.spiegel.de/panorama/gesellschaft/umfrage-in-deutschland-fast-die-haelfte-der-eltern-schlaegt-ihre-kinder-a-820836.html.
109. Könneker, M.-L., *Dr. Heinrich Hoffmanns Struwwelpeter: Unters. zur Entstehungs-u. Funktionsgeschichte e. bürgerl. Bilderbuchs.* 1977: Metzler.
110. Beauchamp, M., Krampus: The devil of Christmas. 2010, San Francisco: Last Gasp. 200.
111. Miller, A. and R.T. Ward, Prisoners of childhood: The drama of the gifted child and the search for the true self. 1981: Basic Books.
112. Scheff, T., Shame and the origins of World War II: Hitler's appeal to German people. Shame and the Modern Self. Melbourne: Australian Scholarly Publishing, 1996.
113. Scheff, T.J. and S.M. Retzinger, Emotions and violence: shame and rage in destructive conflicts. 2002: Backinprint. Com.

REFERENCES

114. Burton, R.V., Honesty and dishonesty. Moral development and behavior. New York: Holt, Rinehart & Winston, 1976: p. 173-197.
115. Burton, R.V., A paradox in theories and research in moral development. Morality, moral behavior, and moral development, 1984: p. 193-207.
116. Kohlberg, L., Moral stages and moralization: The cognitive-developmental approach. Moral development and behavior: Theory, research, and social issues, 1976: p. 31-53.
117. Gilmartin, B.G., The case against spanking. Human Behavior, 1979. **8**(2): p. 18-23.
118. Sears, R.R., H. Levin, and E.E. Maccoby, Patterns of child reading. 1957: Row, Peterson.
119. Gächter, S. and J.F. Schulz, Intrinsic honesty and the prevalence of rule violations across societies. Nature, 2016.
120. Gray, J., The psychology of fear and stress. 1991, Cambridge University Press: Cambridge, UK.
121. Gray, J.A. and N. McNaughton, The neuropsychology of anxiety: an enquiry into the functions of the septo-hippocampal system. 2003, New York: Oxford University Press.
122. Grund, F.J., The Americans, in their moral, social, and political relations. 1837, London: Longman, Rees, Orme, Brown, Green & Longman. 2 v.
123. Salamon, S., Ethnic communities and the structure of agriculture. Rural Sociology, 1985. **50**(3): p. 323.
124. Kluck, P., Decision making among descendants of European farmers in the Rio Grande Do Sul, Brazil. Unpublished Ph. D. Dissertation, Cornell University, Ithaca, New York, 1975.
125. Morris, P.K. and J.A. Waldman, Culture and metaphors in advertisements: France, Germany, Italy, the Netherlands, and the United States. International Journal of Communication, 2011. **5**: p. 27.
126. Flett, G.L., P.L. Hewitt, and D.G. Dyck, Self-oriented perfectionism, neuroticism and anxiety. Personality and Individual Differences, 1989. **10**(7): p. 731-735.
127. Burns, D.D., The perfectionist's script for self-defeat. Psychology Today, 1980. **14**(6): p. 34-52.
128. Byrne, A. and M.W. Eysenck, Individual differences in positive and negative interpretive biases. Personality and Individual Differences, 1993. **14**(6): p. 849-851.

129. Galambos, N.L. and R.A. Dixon, Adolescent abuse and the development of personal sense of control. Child Abuse & Neglect, 1984. **8**(3): p. 285-293.
130. Oates, R.K., D. Forrest, and A. Peacock, Self-esteem of abused children. Child Abuse & Neglect, 1985. **9**(2): p. 159-163.
131. Sonntag, W.a. Psychological Problems. 2012; Available from: http://www.dw.com/en/psychological-problems-force-more-germans-into-early-retirement/a-16488448.
132. Martin, A. and F. Jacobi, Features of hypochondriasis and illness worry in the general population in Germany. Psychosomatic Medicine, 2006. **68**(5): p. 770-777.
133. Boehnke, K., et al., The structure and dynamics of worry: Theory, measurement, and cross-national replications. Journal of Personality, 1998. **66**(5): p. 745-782.
134. Watts, S., L. Dennerstein, and J.D.L. David, The premenstrual syndrome: a psychological evaluation. Journal of Affective Disorders, 1980. **2**(4): p. 257-266.
135. Houston, B.K., Trait anxiety and cognitive coping behavior. Series in Clinical & Community Psychology: Achievement, Stress, & Anxiety, 1982.
136. Jorgensen, R.S. and C.S. Richards, Negative affect and the reporting of physical symptoms among college students. Journal of Counseling Psychology, 1989. **36**(4): p. 501.
137. Barnett, R.C. and G.K. Baruch, Women's involvement in multiple roles and psychological distress. Journal of Personality and Social Psychology, 1985. **49**(1): p. 135.
138. Bleuel, H.P., *Kinder in Deutschland*. 1971: C. Hanser.
139. Nurmi, J.-E. and J. von Wright, Interactive effects of noise, neuroticism and state anxiety in the learning and recall of a textbook passage. Human Learning: Journal of Practical Research & Applications, 1983.
140. Castrillon, F., Translating *Angst:* inhibitions and symptoms in Anglo-American psychoanalysis. European Journal of Psychoanalysis, 2014(July).
141. Perkins, A.M., S.E. Kemp, and P.J. Corr, Fear and anxiety as separable emotions: an investigation of the revised reinforcement sensitivity theory of personality. Emotion, 2007. **7**(2): p. 252.
142. Wierzbicka, A., Emotions across languages and cultures: Diversity and universals. 1999: Cambridge University Press.
143. Wierzbicka, A., *Angst*. Culture & Psychology, 1998. **4**(2): p. 161-188.

REFERENCES

144. Noelle-Neumann, E., The Germans--public opinion polls, 1967-1980. 1981: Greenwood Publishing Group.
145. Orenstein, H., E. Orenstein, and J.E. Carr, Assertiveness and anxiety: A correlational study. Journal of Behavior Therapy and Experimental Psychiatry, 1975. **6**(3): p. 203-207.
146. Johnson, J.A. and F. Ostendorf, Clarification of the five-factor model with the abridged big five dimensional circumplex. Journal of Personality and Social Psychology, 1993. **65**(3): p. 563.
147. Mandler, G. and S.B. Sarason, A study of anxiety and learning. The Journal of Abnormal and Social Psychology, 1952. **47**(2): p. 166.
148. Barron, F., The psychology of the creative writer. Theory Into Practice, 1966. **5**(4): p. 157-159.
149. Parkin, S., The life and death of Petra Kelly. 1994: HarperCollins.
150. Probst, T.M., et al., Productivity, counterproductivity and creativity: The ups and downs of job insecurity. Journal of Occupational and Organizational Psychology, 2007. **80**(3): p. 479-497.
151. Staufenbiel, T. and C.J. König, A model for the effects of job insecurity on performance, turnover intention, and absenteeism. Journal of Occupational and Organizational Psychology, 2010. **83**(1): p. 101-117.
152. Dahrendorf, R., Society and democracy in Germany. 1969, Garden City, N.Y.,: Anchor Books. xvi, 457p.
153. Hirsh, J.B., R.A. Mar, and J.B. Peterson, Psychological entropy: a framework for understanding uncertainty-related anxiety. Psychological Review, 2012. **119**(2): p. 304.
154. Hofstede, G., G.J. Hofstede, and M. Minkov, Cultures and organizations: Software of the mind. Revised and expanded. McGraw-Hill, New York, 2010.
155. Stern, F., National Socialism as temptation. Dreams and delusions. The drama of German history, New York, Knopf, 1987: p. 147-191.
156. Scheuch, E.K., *Die Suche nach der Besonderheit der heutigen Deutschen.* Kölner Zeitschrift für Soziologie und Sozialpsychologie, 1990. **42**(4): p. 734-752.
157. Wilson, G.D., The concept of conservatism. The Psychology of Conservatism (Routledge Revivals), 2013: p. 3.

158. Bouchard, T.J., et al., Evidence for the construct validity and heritability of the Wilson–Patterson conservatism scale: a reared-apart twins study of social attitudes. Personality and Individual Differences, 2003. **34**(6): p. 959-969.
159. Jost, J.T., et al., Political conservatism as motivated social cognition. 2003, American Psychological Association.
160. Wilson, G.D., J. Ausman, and T.R. Mathews, Conservatism and art preferences. Journal of Personality and Social Psychology, 1973. **25**(2): p. 286.
161. Glasgow, M.R., A.M. Cartier, and G.D. Wilson, Conservatism, sensation-seeking and music preferences. Personality and Individual Differences, 1985. **6**(3): p. 395-396.
162. Hall, E.T., The silent language. Vol. 3. 1959: Doubleday: New York.
163. Larson, B., Getting along with the Germans. 1983: Verlag Bechtle.
164. Preiss, G.W., Work goals of engineers: A comparative study between German and US industry. 1971.
165. Fridrich, H.K., A comparative study of US and German middle management attitudes. 1965.
166. Gaspari, C. and H. Millendorfer, *Konturen einer Wende- Strategien für die Zukunft*. 1978: Verlag Styria.
167. Office, U.N.D.P.H.D.R., Human Development Report: Background papers. 1999: Human Development Report Office, United Nations Development Programme.
168. Hall, E.T., The dance of life: The other dimension of time. 1983, New York: Anchor/Doubleday.
169. Hollmann, J., A. de Moura Carpes, and T.A. Beuron, The DaimlerChrysler merger–a cultural mismatch? Revista de Administração da UFSM, 2010. **3**(3): p. 431-440.
170. MacIsaac, D. and U.S.S.B. Survey, The United States Strategic Bombing Survey: a collection of the 31 most important reports printed in 10 volumes. 1976: Garland.
171. Slate, E., Tips for negotiations in Germany and France. HR Focus, 1994. **71**(7 (July)): p. 18.
172. Keese, C., *Silicon Valley: Was aus dem mächtigsten Tal der Welt auf uns zukommt*. 2014: Albrecht Knaus Verlag.
173. Nurge, E., Some depictions of German cultural character, in *The new ethnicity: perpespectives from ethnology*, J.W. Bennett, Editor. 1975, West Publishing St. Paul. p. 217-257.
174. Foster, B., How culture makes a difference in management: Applying Geert Hofstede's cultural dimensions to

REFERENCES

management in Germany and China. 2015, Eastern Michigan University: Ypsilanti. p. 42 p.
175. Hedderich, N., *German-American* inter-cultural differences at the workplace: A survey. Global Business Languages, 2010. **2**(1): p. 14.
176. Schroll-Machl, S., Doing business with Germans: Their perception, our perception. 2013: Vandenhoeck & Ruprecht.
177. Lehmann-Willenbrock, N., J.A. Allen, and A.L. Meinecke, Observing culture: Differences in US-American and German team meeting behaviors. Group Processes & Intergroup Relations, 2013: p.252-271.
178. Kauffeld, S. and N. Lehmann-Willenbrock, Meetings matter effects of team meetings on team and organizational success. Small Group Research, 2012. **43**(2): p. 130-158.
179. Naimark, N.M., The Russians in Germany: a history of the Soviet zone of occupation, *1945-1949*. 1995: Harvard University Press.
180. Hitchcock, W.I., The struggle for Europe: The history of the continent since 1945. 2004: Profile Books.
181. Schwan, H., *Die Frau an seiner Seite: Leben und Leiden der Hannelore Kohl*. 2011: Heyne Verlag.
182. Lilly, J.R., Taken by force: rape and American GIs in Europe during World War II. 2007: Palgrave Macmillan.
183. Overmans, R., *Deutsche militärische Verluste im Zweiten Weltkrieg*. Vol. 46. 2004: Walter de Gruyter.
184. Botting, D., In the ruins of the Reich. 1985: Allen & Unwin.
185. Sorge, M.K., The other price of Hitler's war : German military and civilian losses resulting from World War II. 1986, New York: Greenwood Press. xx, 175 p., .
186. Botting, D., From the ruins of the Reich : Germany, 1945-1949. 1985, New York: Crown. 341 p.
187. Keating, D.P., Born anxious: The lifelong impact of early life adversity-and how to break the cycle. 2017: St. Martin's Press.
188. Susser, E., H.W. Hoek, and A. Brown, Neurodevelopmental disorders after prenatal famine: the story of the Dutch Famine Study. American Journal of Epidemiology, 1998. **147**(3): p. 213-216.
189. Lumey, L. and A.D. Stein, Offspring birth weights after maternal intrauterine undernutrition: a comparison within sibships. American Journal of Epidemiology, 1997. **146**(10): p. 810-819.

190. Kaati, G., L.O. Bygren, and S. Edvinsson, Cardiovascular and diabetes mortality determined by nutrition during parents' and grandparents' slow growth period. European Journal of Human Genetics: EJHG, 2002. **10**(11): p. 682.
191. Yehuda, R., et al., Holocaust exposure induced intergenerational effects on FKBP5 methylation. Biological Psychiatry, 2016. **80**(5): p. 372-380.
192. Perroud, N., et al., The Tutsi genocide and transgenerational transmission of maternal stress: epigenetics and biology of the HPA axis. The World Journal of Biological Psychiatry, 2014. **15**(4): p. 334-345.
193. Harper, L., Epigenetic inheritance and the intergenerational transfer of experience. Psychological Bulletin, 2005. **131**(3): p. 340.
194. Peabody, D. and L.R. Goldberg, *S*ome determinants of factor structures from personality-trait descriptors. Journal of Personality and Social Psychology, 1989. **57**(3): p. 552.
195. Harrington, J.R. and M.J. Gelfand, Tightness–looseness across the 50 united states. Proceedings of the National Academy of Sciences, 2014. **111**(22): p. 7990-7995.
196. Becker, E., The denial of death. 2007, New York: Simon and Schuster.
197. Becker, E., The birth and death of meaning: A perspective in psychiatry and anthropology. 1962: Free Press of Glencoe New York, NY.
198. Greenberg, J., et al., Why do people need self-esteem? Converging evidence that self-esteem serves an anxiety-buffering functio*n*. Journal of Personality and Social Psychology, 1992. **63**(6): p. 913.
199. Pyszczynski, T., et al., Why do people need self-esteem? A theoretical and empirical review. Psychological Bulletin, 2004. **130**(3): p. 435.
200. Yalom, I.D., Existential psychotherapy. 1980: Basic Books.
201. Brauer, M. and N. Chaurand, Descriptive norms, prescriptive norms, and social control: An intercultural comparison of people's reactions to uncivil behaviors. European Journal of Social Psychology, 2010. **40**(3): p. 490-499.
202. Becker, M., et al., Cultural bases for self-evaluation: Seeing oneself positively in different cultural contexts. Personality and Social Psychology Bulletin, 2014. **40**(5): p. 657-675.
203. Greenberg, J., et al., Evidence for terror management theory II: The effects of mortality salience on reactions to those

REFERENCES

who threaten or bolster the cultural worldview. Journal of Personality and Social Psychology, 1990. **58**(2): p. 308-318.
204. Goldenberg, J.L., et al., The body as a source of self-esteem: the effect of mortality salience on identification with one's body, interest in sex, and appearance monitoring. Journal of Personality and Social Psychology, 2000. **79**(1): p. 118.
205. Deschesne, M., J. Greenberg, and J. Schimel, Terror management and sports fan affiliation: The effects of mortality salience on fan identification and optimism. European Journal of Social Psychology, 2000. **30**: p. 815-835.
206. Arndt, J., et al., To belong or not to belong, that is the question: terror management and identification with gender and ethnicity. Journal of Personality and Social Psychology, 2002. **83**(1): p. 26.
207. Sowislo, J.F. and U. Orth, Does low self-esteem predict depression and anxiety? A meta-analysis of longitudinal studies. 2013, American Psychological Association.
208. Scheuch, E.K., *Wie deutsch sind die Deutschen? Eine Nation wandelt ihr Gesicht.* 1992.
209. Eriksson, K., P. Strimling, and J.C. Coultas, Bidirectional associations between descriptive and injunctive norms. Organizational Behavior and Human Decision Processes, 2015. **129**: p. 59-69.
210. Stok, F.M., et al., Don't tell me what I should do, but what others do: The influence of descriptive and injunctive peer norms on fruit consumption in adolescents. British Journal of Health Psychology, 2014. **19**(1): p. 52-64.
211. Gelfand, M.J., et al., Descriptive norms as carriers of culture in negotiation. International Negotiation, 2011. **16**(3): p. 361-381.
212. Gelfand, M.J., L.H. Nishii, and J.L. Raver, On the nature and importance of cultural tightness-looseness. Journal of Applied Psychology, 2006. **91**(6): p. 1225.
213. Gelfand, M.J., et al., Differences between tight and loose cultures: a 33-nation study. Science, 2011. **332**(6033): p. 1100-1104.
214. Hofstede, G. and R.R. McCrae, Personality and culture revisited: Linking traits and dimensions of culture. Cross-Cultural Research, 2004. **38**(1): p. 52-88.
215. McCrae, R.R., et al., Nature over nurture: temperament, personality, and life span development. Journal of Personality and Social Psychology, 2000. **78**(1): p. 173.

216. Allik, J. and R.R. McCrae, A five-factor theory perspective, in *The five-factor model of personality across cultures.* 2002, Springer. p. 303-322.
217. McCrae, R.R., NEO-PI-R data from 36 cultures. The five-factor model of personality across cultures, 2002: p. 105.
218. Angleitner, A. and F. Ostendorf, The German NEO-PI-R: A comparison of German speaking countries (Austria, Germany, former East and West Germany). 2000.

INDEX

abrasiveness, 37
abuse, child, 45, 61
abuse, psychological, 62–63, 62
abuse, sexual, 61
achievement motivation, 21
achievement, need for, 19
action-orientation, 85
Adler, Alfred, 55
administration, 79
admirable and likable nations, 37
agencies, governmental, 83
agendas, 87
aggressions, 15, 16, 60
aggressiveness, 71
agreeableness, 25–26
agreeableness-disagreeableness, 37–43
alcohol, 71
ambiguity, 82
Americans, 26, 31, 78, 86, 88
amygdala, 94
anal fixation, 43–44
anger, 35, 66, 72
Angst: existential, 27; Freud, and, 55; neuroticism, and, 56; Gemütlichkeit:, 38 positive, 72; punishment, and, 59; self-esteem, and, 98; social, 27, 65
apprenticeship, 20
arrogance, 26
art, uncertainty, and, 77

art, order and, 46
assertiveness, 72
ass, lick my, 44
attacks, 9/11, 99
Austria, 91
authoritarianism, 16, 18
authority, questioning, 17
autobahns, 47–48
awareness, lack of, 61
banking, 74
Baron, Frank, 72
Barzini, Luigi, 57
bathrooms, 44
beatings, 60
beer, 45, 68
behavioral activation system (BAS), 56
behavioral inhibition system (BIS), 56
belonging, 98
bias, in ratings, 26
Biesdorf, Heinz, 48
Big Five, 13, listing of, 28–29
Bildung, 51
birthrates, 64
blockade, naval, 92
body, cleanliness, 45
bombing, 84, 92, 93
brainstorming, 89
Brecht, Bertolt, 40
broadmindedness, 64
bureaucratic mentality, 25, 26, 43
Burns, David, 65

busy, keeping, 18, 19
capital, venture, 85
case studies, 85
casualties, war, 92
Catholics, 32, 61, 70
certainties, 75-76
chauvinism, 76
children, crippling from, 47
children, war effects on, 93
Christmas, 75
Chrysler, 77
cleanliness, 43, 45
coal, 11, 13
Commandment, Eleventh, 59
Communist Germany (East), 102
Communists, 76
compartmentalization, 87-88
competition, 74
complaining, 90
compliments, 81
compulsiveness, 62
conditioning, 63
conscientiousness: *Angst*, and, 71; aspects of, 43; culture and, 88; epigenetics and, 94-95; foresight and, 13; frugality and, 13; heritable, 102; norms and, 99; tightness and, 72; traits of, 25, 26; trauma and, 94
consensus, 88
conservatism, 76
context, low, 77-78
control, need for, 33, 34-37
costs, 47-48
courses, management, 79
criticisms, 38, 65, 66, 81
crowds, 34

culture: *Angst*, and, 28; definition of, 73; requirements of, 97
culture/personality intertwined, 95
Culture's Consequences, 73
Daimler, 77
deaths, 97
debt, 13
Decline of the West, 71
deduction (reasoning), 84
defense mechanisms, 55
deficiencies, search for, 39
democracy, 16, 17, 18
Denmark, 91
devils, 69
Diesel, Eugen, 37, 46, 52, 58, 78, 83
dignity, 58
DIN, 84
directness, 80-81, 80
discipline, 17, 91
disorder, 46
disruption, 86
distance, social, 39
doctors, 79
dopamine, 31
dowsing, water, 67
drivenness, dislike of German, 66
Dundes, Alan, 44
Dutch, 94
duties/obligations, 58
East (Communist) Germany, 102
economic power, German, 49
economic success, 49
education, vocational, 20
efficiency, 47-48
efficiency, focus on costs, 47

INDEX

efficiency measurement, 47
ego, screening, 33
Ehrlichman, John, 83
emotions, labile, 57
emotions, words for, 40
engineering, 79, 88
entropy, 74
epigenetics, 94–95
equilibriums, quasi-stationary, 57
Erikson, Erik, 55
escape, from freedom, 70
ethnocentrism, 98
expertise, 78–80
explanations, 84
explicitness, 80
expulsions, 92, 93
extraversion, American vs. German, 31
extraversion-introversion, 25–26
extraverts, 56, 67
extraverts, as uninhibited, 34
faith, 70
faithfulness, 52
family, bounded, 33
famines, 94
farming, 64
father, German, 16, 18
fathers, 57
Faust, 51, 69
fears, 56, 69
Federer, Roger, 64
feelings, bottled up, 34
feelings vs. tasks, 65
fight-flight-freeze-system (FFFS), 56
Financial Stability Facility, 21
fireplaces, 46
firmness, German, 37

First World War, 91
fixation, anal, 43
flexibility, 82
flexibility/persistence, i, 95
foods, healthful, 45
foreigners, 98
forests, 52
France, 11, 12
Franco-Prussian War, 91
frankness, German, 37
French, dislike of, 41
Freud, Sigmund, 16, 43, 55, 68
friendliness, 31, 90
friendships, 33
Fromm, Erich, 55, 69, 70
frugality, 13
funeral, emotions at, 34
future, angst about, 70
Geborgenheit, 75
Gemütlichkeit, 38
Gemütlichkeit, emotions at, 35
General Social Survey, 63, 76
generosity/thrift, 65
Germans, as introverts, 31
Germany: created, 11; power of, economic, 10, 12; splintered, 11; war losses, 11
Germany, East (Communist), 11, 12
Germany, West, annexation of East Germany, 12
Germeinschaft, 39
Gesellschaft, 39
goals, 81, 82, 89
God, 69, 70
Goethe, 37, 51, 52
gold, shitting, 43
Great Britain, 11, 12

Green Party, 68, 72
group decisions, 74
group, focus on, 32
guilt, 62
Haldeman, H.R., 83
Hall, Edward T., 33, 77, 86
hamburger style of criticism, 38
hatred, 40
heads, striking, 60
Heidegger, Martin, 68
Heimat, 75
Hellpacht, Willy, 18, 37, 57
Hertz, Ann, 65
Heuss, Theodor, 41
Hitler, 52; anxieties, and, 55; beatings, and, 61; order, and, 83; as savior, 76; shame, and, 63; terror management, and, 99
Hoffmann, Heinrich, 60
Hofstede, Geert, 73
holidays, 19
honesty, 38, 63, 81, 83, 90
Horney, Karen, 55
humiliations, shaming, 62
humor, 37, 78
hypochondria, 66, 67
identity, search for, 52
immigrants, as extraverted, 32
immortality, 98
incompetence, 80
independence, 97
individualism, 32
infants, comforting of, 97
informality, 80, 81
information, 77
inheritance, 94
initiative, 65

inner-directedness, 52
innovations, 85
insecurities, 56, 57, 58, 72
instability, 27, 57–59
instructions, 78
insurance, 59
interactions, observed, 25
interviews, 25
introversion, 64
introversion, German vs. American, 31
introverts, 67
introverts, and punishment, 59
introverts, as reserved, 34
investments, on farms, 64
inwardness, 51–53
irrationality, 26
Italy, 12
Japan, 86
Jews, 94
jokes, toilet/sex, 43
Jung, Carl, 31
Kadavergehorsam, 53
Kelly, Petra, 72
Kinderfeindlichkeit, 60
Kohl, Hannelore, 92
Krampus, 61
Ladder, Chicken Coop, 44
language, German, 87
Laqueur, Walter, 52, 58, 66
leadership, 79, 89
learning, 59
learning-by-doing, 89
Lebensangst, 66
Lederer, Gerda, 17
legalities, 83
leniency, American, 37
Lenin, Vladimir, 82
Lewin, Kurt, 32, 57

INDEX

liberals, 77
Liebknecht, Karl, 82
lightheartedness, Americans, and 34
love, 53
Luther, Martin, 44, 51, 69–70
male/female ratio, 93
Melanchthon, Philip, 69
Merkel, Angela, 21
methylation, 94
milestones, 89
Milgram, 17
Miller, Alice, 61, 62
mines, coal, 93
mistakes, 39, 80
Mittelstand, 20
modifications, of plans, 89
monochronic cultures, 86–87
mothers, 56, 57, 97
Mozart, 44
music, 77
mutability, 57
My Lai, 17
mysticism, 52
Mytaxi, 85
Napoleon, 15, 41, 91
nationalities, preferences for, 25
Nazis. *See* Hitler
negativism, 65
neuroticism, 26, 28, 102
Nietzsche, Friedrich, 52
Nikolas, St., 61
Nixon, President, 83
noises, 67, 68
norms: prescriptive, 99; social, 98–100; terror management, and, 99; tightness of, 99

norms, cultural, personality vs. 102
nuclear power, 68
nurses, 79
obedience, 16, 17
objective stance, 35
objectivity, 81
obligations/duties, 58
obsessiveness, 44
onion, personality as, 33
openness, 26, 51, 77
order, 46–47; aspects of conscientiousness, 43; need for, 46; rules, and, 82
other-directedness, 32, 52
Pakistan, 99
paralysis through analysis, 88
parents, pleasing, 97
patience, 37
pedagogy, poisonous, 61
pedants, 52
people vs. things, 65
perfectionism, 58, 64–65, 64
performance, 102 conscientiousness and, 48, 49; culture, and, 88; disagreeableness and, 41; introversion/extraversion and, 35; neuroticism, and, 72; traumas, and, 95; without Gemütlichkeit:, 38, free of cognitive abilities, 49
persistence/flexibility, 43
personalities, primacy of, 102
personality/culture intertwined, 73
personality traits, perceived, 25
pessimism, 70, 97

philosophies, 51
photography, 33
planning, 81–84
plans, rigidity of, 89
playgrounds, 60
politeness, 37
politics, right-wing. *See* conservatism
pollution, 68
polychronic cultures, 86
positiveness, 40–41
post-traumatic stress disorder, 92
Potsdam, 93
pragmatism, 85
praise, 65, 80
precedents, 85
precision, 87
predictability, 75
preferences for nationalities, 26–27
presidents, German-American, 76
prison, Stanford, 17
privacy, 32–34
problem analysis, 90
problems, identifying, 88
process, trial-and-error, 89
production, 86
profanity, 44
professors, 51
projects, joint, 88
Protestantism, 31–32
Prussia, 32, 91
public/private behaviors, 38–40
punctuality, 48
punishments, 59–62; anxieties, and, 59; disagreeableness, and, 41;

introverts, and, 32; need for, 63; sensitivity to, 56
quality, product, 80
rapes, 92
rationality, 84–85
Red Army, 92
refugees, 93
regimentation, 62
regulations, 83
Reich, Fourth, 21
research, 84
research, empirical, 79
retirement, 20, 66
reunification, 41
rewards, effective for extraverts, 32
risks, 63, 65
roles, 88
routines, 84
rules, 73, 78, 81–84
safety, 75
Sartre, Jean Paul, 68
schedules, 48
Schmidt (contractor), 66
schoolmasters, 76
science and technology, 47
selectiveness, 64
self-control, 72
self-descriptions, 27
self-esteem, 65, 97
self-improvement, 51
selves, focus on, 32
sensitivities, and pain, 67
sentimentalism, 71
separation anxieties, 56–57, 56
seriousness, 34, 37
serotonin, 56
severity, 59
shame, 62, 63

INDEX

shell shock, 92
shyness, 65
Sicherheit (certainty), 75
signs, traffic, 87
Silicon Valley, 88
sleeping, 59
small-talk, 37
smiles, 39
soap, 45
solutions, 89, 90
Soviet Union, 12
spas, 67
Spengler, Oswald, 71
stability, 58
Stael, Germaine de, 15
starvation, 92, 93
stereotypes, 15–21, 25
stiffness, 76
stock markets, 74
strange situation, 56
strengths, 65
stresses, job, 66
strikes, 20
striving, 57
Struwwelpeter, 60
stubbornness, 57
Stunde Null, 93
superegos, 62
superficiality, 81
Super Shopper Program, 48
surgency, 31
surprises, 81
Sweden, 94
systemization, 84–85
tactfulness, 37
tasks vs. feelings, 38
technology and science, 65
temptations, 63
terrorists, 70
terror management, 97–100

theories, 79
things, and uncertainty 47
things vs. people, 47
Thirty Years' War, 91
threats, 60
threats, environmental, 94
thrift/generosity, 43
thriftiness, 48
tightness, normative, 94
Tillich, Paul, 68
time management, 86
time schedules, 87
Tocqueville, Alexis de, 80, 82
toilet training, 44–46
Tönnies, Ferdinand, 38
too-muchness, 77
training, 89
traits, heritable, 102
traumas, 95
traumas, inheritance of, 94
travels, 46
trust, 81, 87
Uber, 83, 85
Ugly Germans, 40
uncertainties, 77
uncertainty avoidance, 73–75; measurement of, 73, 74; neuroticism, and, 72, 102; planning, and, 81; Silicon Valley, and, 85–86
unions, 75
University Institute, European, 25
vacations, 19–20
values, liberal, 18
values, personal, 98
virtues, private, 51
vocational training, 13
waiting, 48
war, nuclear, 58

THE GERMAN MIND

waste, hatred of, 48
weaknesses, 65
Weltschmerz, 66
Wittgenstein, Ludwig, 40
workaholism, 18, 19
workers, insurance for, 12

work not fun, 90
work, seriousness of, 41
wrong, admit being, 19
"you," German words for, 39

THE AUTHOR

George F. Wieland holds a B.A. in psychology from Stanford University and a Ph.D. in sociology and psychology from the University of Michigan, Ann Arbor. He has taught and conducted research at Michigan, Vanderbilt, and Guy's Hospital Medical School in London, England. He has written several books on hospital and organizational cultures. His latest books on Germans are *Celtic Germans: The Rise and Fall of Ann Arbor's Swabians, Stubborn & Liking It: Einstein & Other Germans in America,* and *Escape from Hell: German Voices.* Originally from New York City, he currently lives in Ann Arbor, Michigan.

Made in the USA
Columbia, SC
07 September 2018